HE CAME DOWN FROM HEAVEN

CHARLES WILLIAMS

WILLIAM B. EERDMANS PUBLISHING COMPANY

GRAND RAPIDS MICHIGAN

© 1938 Michael Williams

First published 1938 by William Heinemann Ltd., London
This edition published 1984 by Wm. B. Eerdmans Publishing Co.
255 Jefferson Ave. S.E., Grand Rapids, MI 49503

Library of Congress Cataloging in Publication Data

Williams, Charles, 1886-1945.
He came down from Heaven.

1. God — Love.   2. Incarnation.   3. Kingdom of God.
4. Love (Theology)   I. Title.
BT140.W55   1984   231′.6   84-13513

ISBN 0-8028-0033-5

CONTENTS

TO

MICHAL

BY WHOM I BEGAN TO STUDY

THE DOCTRINE OF GLORY

Chapter I

Heaven and the Bible

THE word Heaven occurs in the Lord's Prayer twice and in the Nicene Creed three times. The clauses which contain it are: "Our Father which art in heaven"; "Thy will be done on earth as it is in heaven"; "Maker of heaven and earth"; "Who for us men and for our salvation came down from heaven"; "He ascended into heaven". A single sentence, recurrent in the Gospels, is as familiar as these: "The kingdom of heaven is at hand", or more briefly, "The kingdom of heaven."

The Oxford English Dictionary gives various definitions of the word. It is derived from the old English *hefen*. Its earliest meaning is the sky or firmament, the space above the world. It was applied afterwards to the various concentric circles into which that space was supposed to be divided, and presently to the same space considered as "the habitation of God and his angels." Hence, as early as Chaucer, it came to mean a state of spiritual being equivalent to the habitation of divine things, a state of bliss consonant with union with God. Its common meaning to-day, as a religious term, sways between the spiritual and the spatial, with the stress in general slightly, though unintentionally, more upon the second than the first.

This placing of the stress is no doubt due chiefly to the first clause of the Lord's Prayer. That Prayer is more widely known than any of the Creeds, and more habitually used than the phrase from the Gospels. Its opening words undoubtedly imply a place in which "Our Father" exists, a spatial locality inhabited by God. Against this continual suggestion so easily insinuated into minds already too much disposed to it, the great theological definitions of God which forbid men to attribute to him any nature inhabiting place are less frequently found and less effectively imagined. They have to be remembered. But "which art in heaven" is already remembered. Its easy implications have to be refused by attention.

It is not, of course, possible to deny that heaven —in the sense of salvation, bliss, or the presence of God—can exist in space; that would be to deny the Incarnation. But heaven, as such, only exists because of the nature of God, and to his existence alone all bliss is related. In a Jewish tradition God was called "the Place" because all places were referred to him, but he not to any place. With this in mind it might be well that private meditation should sometimes vary the original clause by "Our Father in whom is heaven". The change is for discipline of the mind, for though it is incapable of the apparent superficiality yet it is also incapable of the greater profundity of the

original. That depth prevents another error as
easy as the first and perhaps more dangerous. It
is comparatively easy to train the mind to
remember that the nature of God is not primarily
spatial; it is not quite so easy to remember that
it is not primarily paternal—that is, that he does
not exist primarily for us. No doubt we are, and
can only be, concerned with the way in which he
exists for us. The metaphorical use of the word
way, in its ordinary sense, contains the other.
"I am the way" is no less "I am the way in which
God exists in relation to men" than "I am the
way by which men exist in relation to God". But
there is a distinction between the idea that God
exists primarily for us, and the idea that God
exists primarily for himself. The original opening
of the Lord's Prayer implies that the paternity of
the first two words exists only in the beatitude of
the sixth—"Our Father which art in heaven".
The distinction is not merely pedantic; it encour-
ages in adoration a style of intelligence and
humility. It restores again the lucid contemplation which is epigrammatized in such a phrase as
(Izaak Walton tells us) was loved and used by
John Donne "in a kind of sacred extasie—
*Blessed be God that he is God only and divinely
like himself*".

This heaven which is beatitude is further
defined by the second clause in which the word
occurs in the Lord's Prayer: "Thy will be done
on earth as it is in heaven". It is habitually

assumed that the second part of the clause refers to the beings—angels or other—who possess heaven as a place or are possessed by it as a state. The will that is to be fulfilled on earth is regarded as relating to other events and possibilities than those which are covered in heaven by the will already fulfilled. But in fact there is another possible meaning. The fulfilment of the will in heaven may grammatically relate to us as well as to angels. The events for which we sincerely implore that fulfilment upon earth are already perfectly concluded by it in heaven. Their conclusions have to be known by us on earth, but they already exist as events in heaven. Heaven, that is to say, possesses timelessness; it has the quality of eternity, of (in the definition which Boethius passed on to Aquinas) "the perfect and simultaneous possession of everlasting life". In that simultaneity the passion of the prayer is already granted; all that is left for us to do is to discover in the process of time the conclusion that we have implored in time. "Let us," the clause demands, in this understanding, "know thy will being done upon earth as, in this very event, it is already perfectly done and perfectly known in heaven—in the beatitude which is of thee." This is the consummation of act in belief—in "faith".

Heaven then is beatitude and the eternal fulfil-ment of the Will, the contemporaneousness of perfection. As a state (or a place) in possible relation with us it was created by the Will: "Maker of heaven and earth". But the Creeds which declare this declare also something of the relation. They declare a process, though (it is true) in spatial metaphors: "who for us men and for our salvation came down from heaven. . . . He ascended into heaven". There emerges and returns from that state of eternal beatitude something or someone charged with a particular intention towards men. It is obvious that this must be related to the doing of the Will, because (on the general definition) there is nothing else that can emerge from and return to that state. Of the possibility of that emergence and return, this is not the immediate place to speak. It is obvious that, however we define heaven—spiritually or spatially—the word earth does in fact mean both. Earth is to us inevitably a place, but it is, also inevitably, the only state which we know, our spiritual state within that place. The identification of the two as earth has no doubt assisted us to see both spatial and spiritual meanings in the word heaven. But heaven is distinguished from earth, and earth at the moment may be taken to mean that place and state which have not the eternity of heaven. If it has a perfection, it is a temporal perfection, a perfection known in sequence. The Will emerges from the heaven of its beatitude (and the beatitude of all creatures existing in their mode of perfect relation to it) and returns thither. Of that Will, so emerging and returning, it is said: "The kingdom of heaven is at hand"; it is called "the kingdom of heaven" in that activity.

Religion is the definition of that relationship. The records of it, as it has been understood by Christendom, are contained formally in two sets of documents (i) the Canonical Scriptures: that is, the Bible, (ii) the Rituals of the Church. Neither is complete alone, nor can be understood alone. So far as they can be separated, it might be said that the Bible, up to and including the Acts of the Apostles, is concerned rather with *what happened*, the Rituals with *what is happening*. The Epistles belong to both. It is true that all that did happen is a presentation of what is happening; all the historical events, especially of this category, are a pageant of the events of the human soul. But it is true also that Christendom has always held that the two are indissolubly connected; that the events in the human soul could not exist unless the historical events had existed. If, *per impossibile*, it could be divinely certain that the historical events upon which Christendom reposes had not yet happened, all that could be said would be that they had not *yet* happened. If time and place are wrong, they are at least all that can be wrong. If, by a wild fantasy, the foundations of Christendom are not yet dug, then we have only the architect's plan. But those foundations can never be dug on any other plan. The passion—often the too-angry passion—with which the orthodox have defended a doctrine such as the Virgin Birth has (apart from mystical interpretation and vicious obstinacy) this consummation of the historical sense as its chief cause. The union of history and the individual is, like that of so many other opposites, in the coming of the kingdom of heaven, historic and contemporary at once. It was historic in order that it might always be contemporary; it is contemporary because it was certainly historic.

It is the Bible which describes and defines for us the coming of the kingdom, and by the Bible is meant for this book the English version, the Authorized supplemented by the Revised. It is, whether fortunately or unfortunately, that source from which the English imagination has for centuries received the communication of Christendom, and from which the Christian imagination in England still, commonly and habitually, derives. No doubt this derivation is, to a large extent, governed by the doctrines of the Catholic Church. But it is a fact that most English minds still interested in Christendom regard the Bible and the Church rather as allied and intermingled organisms than the Church as the single organism producing the Bible as a part of its inspired activity. That is why it will be convenient here to follow the complex imagination contained in the phrase "came down from heaven" as it is derived from the Bible. It is the habit nowadays to talk of the Bible as great literature; the Bible-worship of our forefathers has been succeeded by a more misguided and more offensive solemnity of conditioned respect, as accidentally uncritical as deliberately irreligious. Uncritical, because too often that literary respect is oddly conditioned by an ignoring of the book's main theme.

It has certainly many minor themes. Like all the rest of English literature, it consists of a multitude of arrangements of English words expressing, with very great poignancy, various states of being. They are expressed in many different conventions—in narrative, in dialogue, in lyric; in histories, in letters, in schedules and codes of law; in fantasies of apocalypse and myths of creation. Many are familiar enough—the devotion of Ruth, the impatience of Job, the distress of David, the passion of the Shulamite; others are less familiar. The whole of the Bible is a nexus of states of being; a pattern developed in a proper sequence from its bare opening through all its enlarging theme. It even involves states of being more than individual; it concerns itself with corporations and companies. Setting aside supernatural beings, the central figure of the Old Testament is Israel; the central figure of the New is the Church. Those companies dominate their members, except when some peculiarly poignant state of individual being emerges, and by sheer power momentarily dominates the mass. Even then the moment of individuality illuminates and returns to the mass; it is never forgotten that the Israelites are members of the nation as the believers are of the Church, and it is the greater organism which is the full subject, at whatever time. Through those greater organisms, as through the many lesser, there arises a sense of corporate mankind. Individuals and companies, and mankind itself, are all finally set in relation to that non-human cause and centre which is called God.

For the central theme is made up of the lesser themes and of something more, and as in all great literature the lesser themes are there to help compose the greater. The whole Canon signifies a particular thing—the original nature of man, the entrance of contradiction into his nature, and the manner of his restoration. If this theme is ignored the Bible as a whole cannot be understood as literature. By a deprivation of the central idea, and of the personification of that idea, the Bible does not cease to be metaphysics and become literature; it ceases to be anything at all but little bits of literature rather oddly collated. But without that deprivation it is literature related to the greatest of human themes—the nature of man and his destiny. Its doctrine may be wrong, but without its doctrine it is, as a book, nothing. It deals no longer with mankind, as is pretended, only with a number of men. To alter it so may be a moral virtue, but it certainly is not good literary criticism.

Yet it is precisely good literary criticism which is needed, for those of us who are neither theologians, higher critics, nor fundamentalists;

that is, for most of us. We are concerned, if we
are concerned at all, to know what the book is at,
as much as to know what *King Lear* or the *Prelude*
is at, and that can only be done by the methods
of literary criticism, by the contemplation of the
states of being the book describes, by the relation
of phrase to phrase and the illumination of
phrase by phrase, by the discovery (without
ingenuity) of complexity within complexity and
simplicity within simplicity. There is simply no
other way to go about it, because it consists of
words. Bible-reading and meditation must be
based on words; they are meant to extract the
utmost possible meaning out of words. Certainly
there are some books whose words, once we have
studied them, seem to demand from us a moral,
even a metaphysical, assent or dissent. Literary
criticism, that is, may lead to or even be transmuted into something more intense even than
itself. Such books are the *Pilgrim's Progress* and
the *Divine Comedy* and the *De Natura Rerum* and
the Bible. They become something more in the
same way that the crowd around Messias were
suddenly exhibited in an office and authority
unexpected when he looked on them and cried
out "Behold my mother and my brethren". But
that declaration of their maternity did not alter
their original humanity, and so with the words
of these books.

There is, in especial, one law of literary criticism which is of use—the law of emptying the

words. Everyone who has studied great verse
knows how necessary is the effort to clear the mind
of our own second-hand attribution of meanings
to words in order that the poet may fill them with
his meanings. No less care is needed in reading
the Bible. Some form, of course, each word must
retain, some shape and general direction. But its
general colour is, naturally, only learnt from its
use throughout. This has to be discovered. As a
fact words such as "faith", "pardon", or "glory"
are taken with meanings borrowed from the
commonplace of everyday; comparatively few
readers set to work to find out what the Bible
means by them. The word "love" has suffered
even more heavily. The famous saying "God is
love", it is generally assumed, means that God
is like our immediate emotional indulgence, and
not that our meaning of love ought to have
something of the "otherness" and terror of
God.

Acknowledging therefore the general meaning
of a few words as they occur, and even charging
(if desirable) the word heaven when it occurs with
all requisite power, it may be permissible to
examine briefly a few other words and events
contained in the Bible, in relation to the clause
"who . . . came down from heaven". At its
beginning the Bible knows very little of the
meaning of words. All great art creates, as
it were, its own stillness about it, but by the
nature of its subject the Bible does more. It

opens with a single rift of light striking along the darkness which existed before words were: "In the beginning God created the heavens and the earth."

Chapter II

The Myth of the Alteration in Knowledge

THE word "God" in the opening sentences of Genesis is practically characterless. It means only That which creates, and what it creates is good in its own eyes. The diagram of the six days develops with a geometrical precision, measured by the ambiguous word "Day". To give that word the meaning merely of the passage of a myriad years is impossible, so much is it defined by its recurrent evenings and mornings; it is nearer our twenty-four hour day than anything else. Yet time is pressed into it; it has a double relationship of duration, divine and human; and it repeats itself as a refrain of mathematical incantation— the first calculation and the first ritual. Along that rift of light, according to the double pulsing sound—"the evening and the morning were the Day"; "God saw that it was good"—the geometry of creation enlarges. The universe exists, and earth, and the seas, and all creatures. But there is no further explanation of the God.

The heavens are here, no doubt, spatial skies in relation to spatial earth, and the earth is the place of limited perfection in time. Man exists upon earth, and with his appearance the imagination finds that it has abandoned its stand-point at the beginning of that primal ray, and has removed itself to earth. It is the opening of the great myth of man's origins. Earth exists and is good; the man and woman—the Adam—exist and are good; and their whole state is good.[1] It is not less good because there exists a prohibition. But the myth makes use of the prohibition to proceed to its account of the Fall.

There are, roughly, two bases for the idea of the Fall. One is the general Judæo-Christian tradition; the other is the facts of present human existence. Both bases will be rejected by those who have already rejected their fundamental hypotheses. The first depends upon the whole doctrine of the Christian Church, and is a corollary of that doctrine. The second depends upon the hypotheses of an omnipotent and bene-volent God and of man's freewill. "Either there is no Creator (in that sense) *or* the living society of men is in a true sense discarded from his presence", said Newman. Something must have gone wrong somewhere. If (on the hypothesis) it cannot have gone wrong with God, it must have gone wrong with us. If heaven is a name for a state of real perfection, we ourselves have most remarkably "come down from heaven".

[1] There is a reading which takes the "going up of the mist" to be a clouding of creation, after which the separation of the Adam into two creatures took place. But it is not possible in this book to ascend to such speculations. I follow everywhere the most commonplace interpretation.

This necessity of thought has been generally accepted by the Christian Church, though the Church has never defined the nature of that aboriginal catastrophe the tale of which it accepts. It has traditionally rather accepted the view that this catastrophe was the second of its kind, the first having occurred in the "heavens" themselves, and among those creatures whom we call angels. Our own awareness of this explanation is generally referred to the genius of Milton, who certainly shaped it for us in great poetry and made use of it to express his own tender knowledge of the infinite capacity of man's spirit for foolish defiance of the God. But long before Milton the strange tale recedes, and long before Milton the prayers of Christendom implore aid against the malignity of fallen spirits. The popularity of the legend has perhaps been assisted by the excuse it has seemed to offer for mankind, by the pseudo-answer it has appeared to offer to the difficulty of the philosophical imagination concerning a revolt in the good against the good, and by its provision of a figure or figures against whom men can, on the highest principles, launch their capacities of indignant hate and romantic fear. The devil, even if he is a fact, has been an indulgence; he has, on occasion, been encouraged to reintroduce into Christian emotions the dualism which the Christian intellect has denied, and we have relieved our own sense of moral submission by contemplating, even disapprovingly, something which was neither moral nor submissive. An "inferiority complex", in the slang of our day, is not the same thing as humility; the devil has often been the figure of the first, a reverse from the second, and the frontier between the two. While he exists there is always something to which we can be superior.

Of all this, however, the book of Genesis knows nothing (unless, indeed, in the sentence about the mist). The myth of the Fall there is formally limited to the Adam, and to the creature "of the field", an immense subtlety twining into speech. There is not much difference apparently between the Adam and the beasts, except that he (or they) control them. There is nothing about intellectual power; in fact, so far as their activities in Genesis are concerned, the intelligence of the Adam is limited to preserving their lives by obtaining food, by a capacity for agriculture, and by a clear moral sense, though behind these things lies the final incantation of the creation: "Let us make man in Our image, after Our likeness", and the decision upon that, as upon the earliest rift of light: "behold, it was very good".

The nature of the Fall—both while possible and when actual—is clearly defined. The "fruit of the tree" is to bring an increase of knowledge. That increase, however, is, and is desired as being, of a particular kind. It is not merely to know more, but to know in another method. It is primarily the advance (if it can be so called) from knowing good to knowing good and evil; it is (secondarily) the knowing "as gods". A certain knowledge was, by its nature, confined to divine beings. Its communication to man would be, by its nature, disastrous to man. The Adam had been created and were existing in a state of knowledge of good and nothing but good. They knew that there was some kind of alternative, and they knew that the rejection of the alternative was part of their relation to the Omnipotence that created them. That relation was part of the good they enjoyed. But they knew also that the knowledge in the Omnipotence was greater than their own; they understood that in some way it knew "evil".

It was, in future ages, declared by Aquinas that it was of the nature of God to know all possibilities, and to determine which possibility should become fact. "God would not know good things perfectly, unless he also knew evil things . . . for, since evil is not of itself knowable, forasmuch as 'evil is the privation of good', as Augustine says (*Confess.* iii. 7), therefore evil can neither be defined nor known except by good." Things which are not and never will be he knows "not by vision", as he does all things that are, or will be, "but by simple intelligence". It is therefore part of that knowledge that he should understand good in its deprivation, the identity of heaven in its opposite identity of hell, but without "approbation", without calling it into being at all.

It was not so possible for man, and the myth

is the tale of that impossibility. However solemn
and intellectual the exposition of the act sounds,
the act itself is simple enough. It is easy for us
now, after the terrible and prolonged habit of
mankind; it was not, perhaps, very difficult then,—
as easy as picking a fruit from a tree. It was
merely to wish to know an antagonism in the good,
to find out what the good would be like if a
contradiction were introduced into it. Man
desired to know schism in the universe. It was a
knowledge reserved to God; man had been warned
that he could not bear it—"in the day that thou
eatest thereof thou shalt surely die". A serpentine
subtlety overwhelmed that statement with a
grander promise—"Ye shall be as gods, knowing
good and evil". Unfortunately to be as gods
meant, for the Adam, to die, for to know evil, for
them, was to know it not by pure intelligence but
by experience. It was, precisely, to experience
the opposite of good, that is the deprivation of the
good, the slow destruction of the good, and of
themselves with the good.

The Adam were permitted to achieve this
knowledge if they wished; they did so wish. Some
possibility of opposite action there must be if
there is to be any relation between different wills.
Free-will is a thing incomprehensible to the
logical mind, and perhaps not very often possible
to the human spirit. The glasses of water which
we are so often assured that we can or can not
drink do not really refract light on the problem.

"Nihil sumus nisi voluntates," said Augustine, but the thing we fundamentally are is not easily known. Will is rather a thing we may choose to become than a thing we already possess—except so far as we can a little choose to choose, a little will to will. The Adam, with more will, exercised will in the myth. They knew good; they wished to know good and evil. Since there was not— since there never has been and never will be— anything else than the good to know, they knew good as antagonism. All difference consists in the mode of knowledge. They had what they wanted. That they did not like it when they got it does not alter the fact that they certainly got it.

The change in knowledge is indicated by one detail. The tale presents the Adam as naked, and in a state of enjoyment of being naked. It was part of their good; they had delight in their physical natures. There is no suggestion that they had not a delight in their sexual natures and relationship. They had about them a free candour, and that candour of joy was a part of their good. They were not ashamed. They then insisted on knowing good as evil; and they did. They knew that candour as undesirable; they experienced shame. The Omnipotence might intelligently know what the deprivation of that candour would be like, and yet not approve it into existence. The divine prerogative could not enter other beings after that manner; they had to know after their own nature. The thing they had involved confused them, because its nature was confusion. Sex had been good; it became evil. They made themselves aprons. It was exactly what they had determined. Since then it has often been thought that we might recover the single and simple knowledge of good in that respect by tearing up the aprons. It has never, so far, been found that the return is quite so easy. To revoke the knowledge of unlovely shame can only be done by discovering a loveliness of shame (not necessarily that shame, but something more profound) in the good. The Lord, it may be remarked, did not make aprons for the Adam; he made them coats. He was not so sex-conscious as some of the commentators, pious and other.

Another detail is in the interrogation in the garden. It is the conclusion of the first great episode in the myth of origin. The decision has, inevitably, changed the relationship of the Adam to the Omnipotence. It is in the garden and they are afraid. As they have a shameful modesty towards each other, so they have an evil humility towards the Creator. They do not think it tolerable that they should be seen as they are. Unfortunately the interrogation merely exhibits them as they are; a severe actuality is before them, and they dislike it. They know evil; that is, they know the good of fact as repugnant to them. They are forced into it. The well-meaning comment which blames Adam for telling tales about the woman overlooks the fact that he had no choice.

In schools and in divorce-courts we used to be taught to lie on a woman's behalf; the fashion of morals may now have changed. But Adam is not in that kind of divorce-court. He has been dragged out from among the concealing trees of the garden, he is riddled now with a new mode of knowledge, but the old knowledge is forced to speak. The full result of their determination is exhibited. "Ye shall be as gods, knowing good and evil." So you shall. Sorrow and conception; the evil of the ground; the sorrow of life; the hardship of toil; all things in antagonism and schism; love a distress and labour a grief; all the good known in the deprivation of the good, in the deprivation of joy. Only the death which the serpent had derived returns to them as a mercy; they are not, at least, to live for ever; the awful possibility of Eden is removed. They are to be allowed to die.

The contradiction in the nature of man is thus completely established. He knows good, and he knows good as evil. These two capacities will always be present in him; his love will always be twisted with anti-love, with anger, with spite, with jealousy, with alien desires. Lucidity and confusion are alike natural, and there is no corner into which antagonism to pure joy has not broken. It is in the episode of Cain and Abel that this alteration of knowledge is most exhibited. It is shown also in a new development. The original tale had dealt almost wholly with the relation of

the Adam to the Omnipotence; their relation
between themselves had not been much considered. But the next generation sees a schism in
mankind itself. The objection mostly raised to
that episode of the myth is to the sacrifice of the
"firstlings of the flock." It is a natural objection,
and it certainly has to be left unanswered or
answered only by the comment that from beginning to end the Bible is negligent of a great deal
of our humane instincts. Man having got himself
into a state when he was capable of willingly
shedding blood, the shedding of blood could no
longer be neglected. That pouring out of the
blood "which is life" was bound to become a
central thing, for it was the one final and utterly
irrevocable thing. It is that which Adam offers to
the Lord, and which the Lord accepts. Cain
himself seems to have had no humanitarian
objections, or if he had they did not extend to his
relations. But the main point is the first breach in
humanity, the first outrage against *pietas*, and
(more importantly) the first imagined proclamation
of *pietas* from the heavens—from the skies or
from eternal perfection. "Am I my brother's
keeper?" "The voice of thy brother's blood
crieth unto me from the ground. And now art
thou cursed from the earth." Human relationship
has become to a man a source of anger and hate,
and the hatred in its turn brings more desolation.
It is the opening of the second theme of the Bible
—the theme of *pietas* and the community. The

curse of the primeval choice is now fully at work, and the great myth passes on to the first hint of the resolution of the lasting crisis of that curse.

The first book, as it were, of the myth is taken up by the entrance of contradiction into the spirit of man. The second is the period of the covenants. So far there has been no development of the character of the God; not, anyhow, in so many words. It is possible to make deductions, such as to observe Messianic prophecies from the talk of the head and the heel in the garden of Eden, and to discern a careful Providence in the making of coats of skins. But these are rather the drawing of what Wordsworth called "the sustaining thought" from the progress of the tale, and Wordsworth, like any other great writer (even the author, no doubt, of the book of Genesis), distinguished carefully between tales and sustaining thoughts drawn from tales. The second are much more patient of our own interpretations than the first, and there has so far been little interpretation of God in Genesis itself; no more, perhaps, than the implication that he is concerned at the breach of human relations in the murder of Abel. But now—by how little, yet by how much!—there is an alteration. The single rift of pure light in which all that has happened has so far been seen— the identities of heaven and earth, and man setting antagonism in his mind towards them, Adam and Eve passing over the earth, and Cain flying into the wilderness—this lies upon the Flood and changes. The pure light of mere distinction between God and man changes; it takes on colour and becomes prismatic with the rainbow. The very style of the Bible itself changes; the austere opening pulsates with multiplied relationships. Man becomes men.

The first covenant is that with Noah. It begins by repeating the single gift of power with which the Omnipotence had endowed Adam, but it adds to it the threat against Cain, and combines something new of its own. It proclaims a law: "At the hand of every man's brother will I require the life of man." It is a declaration of an exchange of responsibility rather than of joy, but the web of substitution is to that extent created, however distant from the high end and utter conclusion of entire interchange. Into the chaotic experience of good as evil the first pattern of order is intro-duced; every man is to answer for the life of his brother. As the Omnipotence so limits man, it limits itself, and for the first time characterizes itself by a limitation—"the everlasting covenant between God and every living creature of all flesh that is upon the earth." It consents to agreement, to limitation, to patience, patience which is here the first faint hint of a thing yet unknown to the myth, the first preluding check on that activity of power which is presently to become a new mode of power—grace.

The second covenant is that made with

Abraham, and afterwards renewed with Isaac and Jacob. It comes after the destruction of Babel; that symbolic legend of the effort man makes to approach heaven objectively only, as by the vain effort of the removal of aprons. It is a recurrent effort, since it is a recurrent temptation: if this or that could be done, surely the great tower would arise, and we should walk in heaven among gods— as when the orthodox of any creed think that all will be well when their creed is universal. Yet the recurrent opposite is no more true, for unless something is done, nothing happens. Unless devotion is given to a thing which must prove false in the end, the thing that is true in the end cannot enter. But the distinction between necessary belief and unnecessary credulity is as necessary as belief; it is the heightening and purifying of belief. There is nothing that matters of which it is not sometimes desirable to feel: "this does not matter." "This also is Thou; neither is this Thou." But it may be admitted also that this is part of the technique of belief in our present state; not even Isaiah or Aquinas have pursued to its revelation the mystery of self-scepticism in the divine. The nearest, perhaps, we can get to that is in the incredulous joy of great romantic moments—in love or poetry or what else: "this cannot possibly be, and it is." Usually the way must be made ready for heaven, and then it will come by some other; the sacrifice must be made ready, and the fire will strike on another altar. So much Cain saw, and could not guess that the very purpose of his offering was to make his brother's acceptable.

Babel had fallen, and the nations and peoples of the earth were established, in variation of speech and habit like the rainbow of the covenant above them. Out of that covenant a new order issues, and the first great formula of salvation. It is the promise and first establishment of Israel, but of Israel in a formula which applies both to it and to the future company of the New Testament, the Church. "I will bless thee . . . thou shalt be a blessing . . . in thee shall all families of the earth be blessed" (Gen. xii. 1–3). Israel is to be exclusive and inclusive at once, like all modes of redemption, particular and universal. Their inclusive-exclusive statement is retained in the repetitions of the covenants, and it is permitted to become indeed a covenant. The covenant with Noah had been rather a one-sided promise than a covenant, but now a sign is established. Besides the exchange of responsibility, the *pietas* between man and man, there is to be a particular mode of adoration, ritual and deliberately ritual. It is the exclusive sign which is to be inclusive in its effects. The uncircumcized child is to be cut off from the people, yet all the earth is again to know beatitude. The mysterious promise of blessing is to be established in that intimate body of man which had, in the old myth, swallowed the fatal fruit: "my covenant shall be in your flesh." The precise declaration is renewed to the generations; the single is to be a blessing to all.

There are two points here which may be remarked in the mere manner of the myth. The first relates to what are usually called the anthropomorphic appearances of the God. There is no doubt that they happen, but the point is that they are precisely appearances. They are rare, and they are condescensions. They succeed in their effectiveness because they are unusual condescensions. The God of Genesis is not a kind of supernatural man; he is something quite different which occasionally deigns to appear like a supernatural man. Something unlike man behaves like man. It exists; it breaks off. "And the Lord went his way . . . and Abraham returned unto his place."

The second point refers to a question of style. The climax of those anthropomorphic appearances is in that most admirably composed passage of words with Abraham concerning Sodom. Up to then the few conversations between man and the Omnipotence have been extremely one-sided. But now there appears something new: the conversation becomes a dialogue. The remoteness and rigour of the Lord take on a tenderness— almost (but for the terror of the subject) a laughter—and there exists not only a promise but a reply. The promise, that is, becomes a fuller and richer thing; it is the whole meaning of prayer. Prayer, like everything else, was meant for a means of joy; but, in our knowledge of the good as evil, we have to recover it so, and it is not an easy thing. Prayer is thought of as a means to an end, but the end itself is sometimes only the means to the means, as with all love. The fantastic intercession of Abraham dances and retreats and salaams and dances again; and the thunder that threatens on the left the Cities of the Plain murmurs gently on the right above the tents. "And the Lord went his way."

The myth draws to a conclusion with what may, or may not, be a beginning of history, and yet at that beginning renews its full splendour of style. The last great outbreak of legend is laid among recognizable peoples and familiar titles. Kings and wizards, priests and prophets, caravans and armies, rich men and slaves, are habitual upon earth; something infinitely various is to be offered to the Lord. Such individual moments as the passion of Jacob for Rachel or of Rebekah for Jacob appear; though the numinous appearances linger, as in the figure that strives with Jacob. The inclusive-exclusive thing is followed in its wanderings among the other existences, who do not know it and are to be blessed through it. But now something else has developed on the earth, the impiety of which Cain was the first incarnation. The development of man into peoples has developed also the dark fact of contradiction, and the law of exchange of responsibility is now outraged nationally as well as individually. The rejection of

Joseph by his brethren expands into the slavery of the Israelites among the Egyptians. Impiety has reached through the whole social order, and the power of tyranny is established as an accepted thing in the world. It is exceptionally, in this instance, related to the "chosen people," the means of returning beatitude, and it is in relation to the same people that, in the midst of so much evil still preferred, the God characterizes himself still farther. He utters the first grand metaphysical phrase: the "I am that I am." Coleridge, as a poet as well as a philosopher, declared that it should be: "I am in that I am." But the alteration is sufficiently given in the message to Pharoah: "the I am hath sent me unto you." The colours of the rainbows are assumed again into a clear light, and the God is no longer only creative but self-existent. It is this utter self-existence the sound of which is prolonged now through the whole book; "I am the Lord" rings everywhere like the refrain of the heavens.

The first work of that declared self-existence is to free the inclusive-exclusive thing upon earth; indeed, it proclaims itself in the course of that freeing. There emerges at that moment a thing of which Christendom has never lost the vision or the tradition—revolution. The tale of it here may be incredible; it may even be disbelieved. The launching of the plagues on the land of Egypt, the hardening of the heart of Pharoah into the thing that Pharoah himself has wished, the locusts and the frogs and the Nile as blood—all these may be the romantic decorations of the legend. In effect the answer of Pharoah is common enough: "We will chance all that rather than let the people go"—till the dead lie in the streets of the cities. The vision of those streets has remained. In the night of death, when all the hopes and heirs of Egypt lie motionless, the victims of impiety are redeemed. The dispossessed and the rejected are in movement through the whole land. Renounce the myth and the vision remains. There is flung out for us the image of the great host, bribed and adorned with the jewels of their taskmasters, marching out under the prophet and the priest and the woman; marching under the fire and the cloud of the terrible covenanted God. "I am that I am"; "I am the Lord." The heavens go before the host, the habitation of the proceeding Power, and of the single voice in and beyond creation that is able to proclaim its own identity, the voice of the original good. They pour on; the waters stand up to let them pass, and nature is hurled back for the departure of the slaves. "Why callest thou upon me? speak unto the children of Israel that they go forward." It is the law of exchange that advances, of the keeping of one life by another, of the oath that cannot be controlled by man; it is the knowledge of good as good breaking out of the knowledge of good as evil. "The Egyptians shall know that I am the Lord when I have gotten me honour upon Pharoah, upon his chariots, and upon his horsemen." In a symbol of universal application, the angel of the Lord and the cloud of heaven stand between the two hosts, and between the two methods of knowledge, and the sea roars down. In the morning the chariots and bodies of the dead are tossed on the shore, and the timbrels of the singing women mock at the wreckage of the possessors and the rich, while the shout of the free people adores the Divine salvation.

Chapter III

The Mystery of Pardon and the Paradox of Vanity

IT is perhaps worth pausing before considering certain aspects of the Prophets, upon another book of the Old Testament. Between the group of books which is mainly mythical and historic and the group which is mainly lyric and prophetic lies, at the centre of the Old Testament, the book of Job. The book of Job, as every one knows owing to the popularity of the Bible as literature, is a very remarkable work. There seems to be a general indefinite opinion that it only got into the Bible by accident, and that its author would be astonished and perhaps ashamed if he could know his companions. Certainly it is thought that the author of most of the book would be ashamed of the author of the last chapter, who provided Job with a happy ending, much as Shakespeare provided reckless marriages—the official equivalent of a happy ending—in so many of his last acts.

At the risk of contumely, however, it remains possible to consider Job as an English book. The adept critics may object, but hardly anyone else dare, for fear a little further criticism should

undercut their own position. For the author of the
last chapter added one important thing to the
Bible, a thing implicit in the rest of Job and indeed
in much else of the Bible, but hardly so adequately
defined anywhere else—except indeed by the
Virgin Mary. His work has saved Christendom
from being misled by St. Paul's rash refusal to
allow the thing formed to ask questions of him
that formed it, the pot of the potter: one of those
metaphors which miss the bull while thudding the
target, like the often-repeated comparison between the Church and a club. No club (however
Right or however Left or however Central—not
even the Sodality of St. Thomas Didymus,
Apostle and Sceptic) claims to be possessed of the
only certain means of salvation. No pot—so far—
has asked questions of the potter in a voice the
potter can understand; when it does, it will be
time enough to compare pots to men. The
criticism is not aimed at St. Paul who dropped the
phrase in the midst of a great spiritual wrestle,
not as a moral instruction. But it has been used
too often by the pious to encourage them to say,
in love or in laziness, "Our little minds were
never meant . . ." Fortunately there is the book
of Job to make it clear that our little minds were
meant. A great curiosity ought to exist concerning
divine things. Man was intended to argue with
God.

It is an odd comment on our reading of original
texts (and not only the text of the Bible) to

remember that one of the commonest phrases in the language attributes patience to Job. Any reader who, with that in his mind, turns to the words which Job actually utters will find that, after a single rebuke to his wife for advising him to curse God, he plunges into a series of demands on and accusations of God which may be and indeed are epigrams of high intelligence, but are not noticeably patient. It is indeed his impatience which his friends find shameful in him. He who has been not only a prince of this world, but also in his righteousness almost a prince of heaven, who has not only served God himself but has intereded for others, whose tragedy has conformed (though they could not know it) almost to Aristotle's rules, ruins both Greek form and Jewish piety by hurling accusations against the Immortal. He does not merely blame God on his own behalf; he denounces God's way with mankind.

An analysis of the whole book has been supplied often enough, and in default of any convenient analysis there is even the book itself to be read. The first point here is the bitterness of the accusation: "He will laugh at the trial of the innocent"; "is it good unto thee that thou shouldest oppress?"; "he removeth away the speech of the trusty, and taketh away the understanding of the aged." The second is the demand for some kind of equality: "Let him take away his rod from me, and let not his fear terrify me, then

would I speak and not fear him"; "O that I knew
where I might find him! that I might come even
to his seat! I would order my cause before him,
and fill my mouth with argument"; "behold, my
desire is, that the Almighty would answer me."
If God will make himself man's equal—so, if not,
there is no sense in talking. Let him submit
himself to question, but does he? no; "he taketh
away the understanding of the aged."

The stark rage of Job produces, in the pause
that follows the whole argument, an answering
rage in the universe; there breaks out of the air
about the disputants a storm of taunts. The air
itself is twisted and swept into a whirlwind, as if
something within it drove outwards; an effect
rare but magnificent in literature, as when Dante
in the Earthly Paradise sees lights that seem to
emerge from within the air rather than to advance
through it. The veil of creation dissolves, and the
images worked on it become living and doubly
mighty in the voice that summons them. The
Lord declines altogether to withdraw his hand or
to modify his nature. He speaks irrationally; he
offers no kind of intelligent explanation. But the
main point is that he has answered; he has ack-
nowledged Job's claim even if only to rail at it.
His mockeries are themselves a reply. It is true
he says nothing new—nothing that Job has not
already said. "Canst thou bind the sweet in-
fluences of Pleiades, or loose the bands of Orion?
canst thou bring forth Mazzaroth in his season?

or canst thou guide Arcturus with his sons?"
Except for Mazzaroth, the Lord is only plagiariz-
ing here from Job, who had already said of him:
"which maketh Arcturus, Orion, and Pleiades,
and the chambers of the south." The whole force
of the conclusion is in the fact that it is a reply.

But the reply is not confined to Job. The three
friends who have been defending orthodoxy and
assuring Job of his sinfulness have their reward.
"Ye have not spoken of me the thing that is right
as my servant Job hath." Job is to sacrifice and
intercede for them, "lest I deal with you after
your folly." The pretence that we must not ask
God what he thinks he is doing (and is therefore
doing) is swept away. The Lord demands that his
people shall demand an explanation from him.
Whether they understand it or like it when they
get it is another matter, but demand it they must
and shall. Humility has never consisted in not
asking questions; it does not make men less
themselves or less intelligent, but more intelligent and more themselves. "And the Lord
turned the captivity of Job, when he prayed for
his friends; also the Lord gave Job twice as much
as he had before." It is the intercession, then,
which marks the moment of return; the salvation
of Job from his distress is at the time of interchange. But it was Job's philosophical impatience of angry curiosity that brought him to
such a moment. Such a philosophical curiosity is
carried on into the New Testament. It accom-

panies the Annunciation. The Blessed Virgin
answered the angelic proclamation with a question:
"How shall these things be?" And of the in-
habitants of heaven themselves it is said that
"these things the angels desire to look into."

The whirlwind of Job is related to another
exposition of the heavens—the darkness and fire
of Sinai. Sinai in the Bible is the conclusion of the
legends and the beginning of the laws. Moses
went up into the Mount as myth; descended as
moral teacher. He was a leader in both periods,
but there was a difference—as there is a difference
in the God to whom he went and the people to
whom he returned. The vision of the people as a
host marching does not preclude the vision of the
people as a mere mob, and it is the mob who
become manifest during the dwelling of Moses in
the Mount. It is the aggregate of uncertain
multitudes and uncertain men; it sways to and
fro. This change of value repeats itself continually
in the history of the children of Israel.[1] It is that
change and change back which are responsible for
the recurrent phrase "the Lord repented him,"
which is nonsense and truth at once. It is, as a
phrase, the continuation of the dialogue with
Abraham, the promise as a reply; the prelude of
something yet deeper and still to be; the hint of the

---

[1] Any book which has occasion to refer often to the
Israelites must feel the need of some kind of apology to the
Jews. No Englishman could be expected to enjoy such a
continual easy discussion of his forefathers by minds of a
different culture, and no apology can quite excuse it. Even
its inevitability hardly does so.

self-limitation of the first covenant carried on to the subordination of the far East. The Will of the Omnipotence is to be turned aside and to submit itself. "The Lord repented him."

But while the people become the mob, the idea of the people is illuminated in the Mount. On the arrival at Sinai the salvation of Israel is defined: "Ye shall be unto me a kingdom of priests and an holy nation." It is one of the great dreams—a people, a nation, a city, a group, any community great or small—a world of intermediaries, communicating to each other the holy and awful Rites, and yet those Rites (in that state of being) no stranger than common things; the ordinary and extraordinary made extraordinary and ordinary by joy. The means of the coming of this kingdom of priests is in the law, and the law is a movement towards the reconciliation of the divided knowledge, the expulsion of the contradiction from man's nature, the discovery once more of the good as pure good. The I AM (and indeed all life) is experienced in an evil manner, but the I AM has sworn that he and it shall be known as good, and only good, to whoever chooses. The first step is the re-creation of an order in the confusion, so that a more than social distinction shall be made. It is important to maintain the *pietas* towards man, but no less the acknowledgment and adoration of the complex thing of heaven.

It is this law and the covenant of which it is a part which the prophets, later, guard. They are

the keepers of the contract; they preserve the
relations of the I AM with the people. They
preserve also the vision of the glory of the I AM.
The word glory, to English ears, usually means no
more than a kind of mazy bright blur. But the
maze should be, though it generally is not, exact,
and the brightness should be that of a geometrical
pattern. It is this which becomes a kind of key
problem—what is the web of the glory of heaven
as a state? It may be said, roughly, that certain
patterns in the web are already discernible: the
recognition of the good, everywhere and always, as
good, the reflection of power, the exercise of
intellect, the importance of interchange, and a
deliberate relation to the Centre. All this is
knowledge of good, knowledge of joy, and not
only a mental knowledge (though it includes that)
but a knowledge through every capacity of being.
Heaven, one may say, has been (apart from its
spatial meaning) hitherto not much more than the
mere exposition of the I AM; first a rift of light,
then a prism of the colours of divine goodwill,
then a light of metaphysical existence. On Sinai
the glory is precisely the brightness of that
existence radiated outward. Moses, in a cleft of
the rock, entreats to see the glory, and beholds the
God pass by: "I will make all my goodness pass
before thee . . . thou canst not see my face: for
there shall no man see me and live." The glory is
the goodness, but even the goodness is not
he.

Moses saw it, as it were, simply. Isaiah and Ezekiel see more. In the sixth chapter of the one, and the first of the other, the undifferentiated glory of Sinai has become living complexes of radiancy. The monsters of earth in Job are rivalled in the prophets by monsters of heaven. "Above it stood the seraphim: each one had six wings; with twain he covered his face, and with twain he covered his feet, and with twain he did fly." "As for the likeness of the living creatures, their appearance was like burning coals of fire, and like the appearance of lamps; it went up and down among the living creatures; and the fire was bright, and out of the fire went forth lightning. And the living creatures ran and returned as the appearance of a flash of lightning. . . . The appearance of the wheels and their work was like unto the colour of a beryl . . . as it were a wheel in the middle of a wheel." "As for their rings they were so high that they were dreadful, and their rings were full of eyes." "And the likeness of the firmament upon the heads of the living creatures was as the colour of the terrible crystal, stretched forth over their wings above."

The wheels and the eyes, and the spirit in the wheels, and their lifting up, have been subject to a good deal of gay humour, but they are a myth of a vital pattern of organisms. "God always geometrizes" said Plato, and the Hebrew prophets thought no less. There is something more also; round the appearance of a throne and "the

likeness as the appearance of a man above upon
it" (anthropormorphic creatures!) is the old
prism of promise. The likeness as the appearance
of the man is "as the colour of amber, as the
appearance of fire round about within it" upward
from the loins, and downward from "the appearance" of loins is the appearance of fire "and it had
brightness round about. As the appearance of the
bow that is in the cloud in the day of rain, so was
the appearance of the brightness round about.
This was the appearance of the likeness of the
glory of the Lord. And when I saw it I fell upon
my face . . . and he said unto me, Son of man,
stand upon thy feet, and I will speak with thee."

The colours of the rainbow had been a witness
to the covenant; now they are the accompaniment
of that which rides upon the bright mathematics of
the company of heaven. Any presentation more
reluctant to become anthropomorphic—with its
likenesses and its appearances, and its obvious
insistence upon them as similes and metaphors—
can hardly be imagined. Since of course in the
end anything that means anything to man has to
be in terms of something remotely significant to
man, from the wheels of Ezekiel to the vortices of
pure thought of Mr. Shaw or the monstrous
equations of great science. It is true that in some
way or other those earlier mathematics profess a
relation to man. On that final grand division there
can, it seems, be no compromise; either the Lord
is concerned with man in himself or he is not. It

is for man to make a fair return by an adoration of the Lord only in himself.

The prophets are sent out from the visible mathematics of the glory to proclaim the moral mathematics of the glory. Morality is either the mathematics of power or it is nothing. Their business is to recover mankind—but first the inclusive-exclusive Israel—to an effort to know only the good. This, in effect, means recognition of the covenant, and obedience to the law. Those who refuse are described in language which precisely carries on the definition of the contradiction involved in the original Fall. "Woe unto them that call evil good and good evil . . . that are wise in their own eyes and prudent in their own sight." The Adam had desired to share the knowledge of the God; they had wished to experience good as something else than good, to discover a hostility in the good. So they did. Their descendants, in the situation in which they were involved, had (and have) the same choice. They can prolong the Fall by their will. They can introduce their own prudence and wisdom into the nature of the good. It is something deeper than impiety or immorality, though it involves them. It is the preference of their own wisdom; it is sin.

Sin has many forms, but the work of all is the same—the preference of an immediately satisfying experience of things to the believed pattern of the universe; one may even say, the pattern of the glory. It has, in the prophets as everywhere, two chief modes of existence: impiety against man and impiety against God—the refusal of others and the insistence on the self.

The first of these here is the consent to social injustice, and the personal gain through social injustice. The people which were brought out of slavery in Egypt have deliberately "called evil good." The prophets—at most times—use more effective language than the abstract "social injustice." What they say is expressed by Amos:

"Hear this, O ye that swallow up the needy, even to make the poor of the land to fail,

"Saying, When will the new moon be gone, that we may sell corn? and the sabbath, that we may set forth wheat, making the ephah small, and the shekel great, and falsifying the balances by deceit?

"That we may buy the poor for silver, and the needy for a pair of shoes; yea, and sell the refuse of the wheat?"

This failure in the communion of justice ruins all the relations between the I AM and the people. Where the oppressed go unrelieved and the princes follow after rewards, the power of the heavens is turned against man, and no kind of adoration will appease it: "bring no more vain oblations; incense is an abomination . . . it is iniquity, even the solemn meeting. Your new moons and your appointed feasts my soul hateth . . . your hands are full of blood." Nevertheless

the communion of justice is not sufficient in itself;
it is to be perfected by adoration. It is man's
business not merely to set up a covenant between
himself and his brother, to maintain the exchange
of responsibility between life and life, but also to
keep the covenant between himself and that other
mode of being which can only be signified by the
fire of amber above the prismatic brightness of
heaven. The two kinds of life are to come
together. But this other can also be rejected.
There is perhaps no better description of this
rejection than is given by Ezekiel.

"And he brought me to the door of the court;
and when I looked, behold a hole in the wall.

"Then said he unto me, Son of man, dig now
in the wall: and when I had digged in the wall,
behold a door.

"And he said unto me, Go in, and behold the
wicked abominations that they do here.

"So I went in and saw; and behold every form
of creeping things, and abominable beasts, and
all the idols of the house of Israel, portrayed
upon the wall round about.

"And there stood before them seventy men of
the ancients of the house of Israel, and in the
midst of them stood Jaazaniah the son of Shaphan,
with every man his censer in his hand; and a
thick cloud of incense went up.

"Then said he unto me, Son of man, hast thou
seen what the ancients of the house of Israel do in
the dark, every man in the chambers of his

imagery? for they say, The Lord seeth us not; the Lord hath forsaken the earth."

The digging in the wall and the discovery of the secret chamber, the thick incense before the images of creeping things on the wall, the old men swinging thuribles before the shapes of abominable beasts—all this is a significance of choice in terms of adoration. So the rich men waiting for the end of the ritual feasts to trick the markets, to entrap the poor and throw them a few clothes for their lives' labour, to defraud them even then by selling refuse in the place of food—this is a significance of choice in terms of justice. Either way there is the preference of a lie, a desired contradiction, a calling of evil good. It is summed up in Jeremiah: "a wonderful and horrible thing is committed in the land; the prophets prophesy falsely, and the priests bear rule by their means; and my people love to have it so; and what will ye do in the end thereof?"

The denunciations of this evil are intervolved all through with exhortation, appeal, and promise. The God of fury is a God of reconciliation also, a whirlwind of anger and promise. Man can turn, repent, do well, recognize good as good and evil as evil. It is perhaps natural to the prophets that they should show very little consciousness of the fact that conversion, repentance, and a new life are not the easiest things. They put it, as many saints have done, on almost purely intellectual grounds: "Come now and let us reason together,

saith the Lord." The lucidity of "I am that I am"
is to be carried into all relations. Surely the thing
is clear enough: do this, and all will be well, your
sin shall be pardoned. They allow for the fact
that people want to sin, but they find it difficult to
believe that people do not also want to be intelligent, and since, on their hypothesis, there is
no doubt what intelligence involves, they become
angry when Israel remains obdurate. That
obstinacy in the eyes of the prophets is levelled
against something clear and simple, and terrible
and complex: a little child leading leopards and
lions, lambs and calves, no hurt and no
destruction; the peace and the bliss of heaven
communicated again in the natural good of earth.

If however the obstinate heart is turned, it is to
find mercy and pardon. "I, even I, am he that
blotteth out thy transgressions for mine own sake,
and will not remember thy sins." The act of
pardon is an act of oblivion. The appeal of the
repentant is for the same forgetfulness: be
tender, forget the evil, remember the good! In the
great prayer of Solomon at the opening of the
temple the cry strikes up continually: "hear thou
in heaven thy dwelling-place, and when thou
hearest forgive." Heaven is to be the place and the
state of the setting aside of the sin that has been
committed. But forgetfulness implies a temporal
state; there can be no eternal oblivion of an act
of which there is an eternal awareness, and the
very nature of eternity is awareness of all: "the

perfect and simultaneous possession of everlasting life."

The prophets are too much concerned with their demand for penitence and their message of pardon to have time for metaphysics. They allow this anthropomorphism—more serious, because more philosophical—to pass. The fiery and amber likeness of the appearance of a man is not likely to deceive many hearers of Ezekiel, but the idea that the Lord is of time is more dangerous. But Ezekiel and his companions are no more concerned with a metaphysical analysis of the absolute than they are with a defence of the myths of a condescended apparition. They are hammering at the heart. Heaven to them is not so much of eternity as it is of the specious present— the present in which there is time to do things about the past and future, to reason, to repent, to redeem. Yet the reader who, by his detachment or his frowardness, can escape the hammer of their command, the chisel of their entreaty, is left with the problem still in his mind: how can the High and Holy One forget? how can he refuse to know what has been? how can the eternity of heaven exclude from itself the knowledge of man's knowing good in schism, and of good as evil? how can the Lord forgive? In what possible sense can the deeds that are as scarlet be as white as snow, and those that are crimson as wool? And if the indescribable Omnipotence could, then what of man? can he only find felicity by losing fact? It is

not conceivable that Omniscience should forget;
it is not satisfactory that the redeemed should
forget. If a corner of experience is to be hidden,
the unity is by so much impaired.

The problem is left unanswered. It has indeed
only been raised because of the appearance in the
heavens of this new quality—say, rather, of this
new word. The truth is that the word is not yet
defined. We think it is already clear because we
impart into it our second-rate meanings. We have
some justification. The Lord is presented in effect
as saying: "Well, We will say no more about it";
or (more shockingly): "Well, We forgive you on
condition that you don't do it again." The
condition in these books is a little too obviously
prevalent. Blake answered it out of man's heart:

> Doth Jehovah forgive a debt only on condition
>   that it shall
> Be payed? Doth he forgive pollution only on
>   conditions of purity?
> That debt is not forgiven! That pollution is
>   not forgiven!
> Such is the forgiveness of the gods, the moral
>   virtues of the
> Heathen whose tender mercies are cruelty.

He proceeded to define pardon in another
sense; to quote it would be to import meanings.
It is enough here to leave the word undefined,
for if the meaning of pardon (beyond forgetfulness) is obscure, yet the method of the re-

demption is, to an extent, comprehensible. There are three principal suggestions.

(1) The first is given most clearly in Jeremiah (xxxi. 33–4) where the Omnipotence declares that a new contract is to be made with the inclusive-exclusive thing. It is to be different from the old contract, which Israel has broken. "This shall be the covenant."

"I will put my law in their inward parts, and write it in their hearts; and will be their God, and they shall be my people. And they shall teach no more every man his neighbour, and every man his brother, saying, Know the Lord: for they shall all know me, from the least of them unto the greatest of them, saith the Lord, for I will forgive their iniquity, and I will remember their sin no more."

The first point of covenant is the making an inward thing of the law. It is to be no longer a thing known and obeyed by a difficult decision; it is to become an instinct, a natural desire of body and spirit. The doctrine is to be known universally through the people, so that no-one is to teach it or be taught, for all that remains is the practice, the practice of restored good: "Ye have seen . . . how I bore you on eagles' wings and brought you unto myself . . . ye shall be unto me a kingdom of priests and an holy nation." Intercommunication of instinctive good everywhere; good no more known in any sense as evil; restoration of humility, of sanctity, of joy.

(2) Nor is the restoration to be limited to Israel; the purpose of Israel is to be fulfilled through the universal earth. "The isles shall wait for his law"; "my name shall be great among the Gentiles." The law that is to be written within is to be written everywhere: instinctive as the heart, broad as the earth.

(3) All the evil is to be forgotten. Within and without, present and past, the world is to know good as good, and to practise it between themselves. There is however one group of passages which, relating to this promise and change, have about them a difference. They are what are called the Servant Songs of Isaiah. They are generally supposed to consist of the following passages: xlii, 1–4, xlix, 1–6, l, 4–9, lii 13— liii 12. They are, of course, regarded now as Messianic, but that is not here the point. There is in them a common element—a figure called "my servant" or more simply "He." This He is the servant and elect of the Lord. He is to be the means of spreading the restoration to the Gentiles (though he is sometimes spoken of as Israel); he is to be, that is, himself an example of the inclusive-exclusive formula. He is as terrible as weapons— swords or arrows; he is to become an astonishment to men; he is to be exalted. But the riddle of his nature reaches its extreme point in the 53rd chapter. There, for the first time, another principle of exchange is hinted. In the early covenant one man was to be responsible for the

life of another. Here however is another kind of substitution, in the midst of passages of joy and beatitude—"Awake, awake; put on thy strength, O Zion"; "Sing, O barren, thou that didst not bear"; "their righteousness is of me, saith the Lord"; "Ho, every one that thirsteth, come ye to the waters." This substitution is of a vicarious suffering and success. It is unique in the Old Testament, yet it is in accord with both the law and the promise. It is certainly not here explained.

"For he shall grow up before him as a tender plant, and as a root out of a dry ground: he hath no form nor comeliness; and when we shall see him, there is no beauty that we should desire him.

"He is despised and rejected of men; a man of sorrows, and acquainted with grief: and we hid as it were our faces from him; he was despised, and we esteemed him not.

"Surely he hath borne our griefs, and carried our sorrows: yet we did esteem him stricken, smitten of God, and afflicted.

"But he was wounded for our transgressions, he was bruised for our iniquities: the chastisement of our peace was upon him; and with his stripes we are healed.

"All we like sheep have gone astray; we have turned every one to his own way; and the LORD hath laid on him the iniquity of us all.

"He was oppressed, and he was afflicted, yet

he opened not his mouth: he is brought as a
lamb to the slaughter, and as a sheep before her
shearers is dumb, so he openeth not his mouth.

"He was taken from prison and from judgment:
and who shall declare his generation? for he was
cut off out of the land of the living: for the
transgression of my people was he stricken."

These then are the main points of the restored
life, as far as the prophets know it. The new
knowledge is to lose from it the recollection of past
sin; it will be remembered neither in heaven nor
on earth; the kingdom of the Lord is free from it.
The new knowledge again is to be instinctive and
natural, a lovely habit, a practice of joy; it will not
need instructors and officiants, because all will
officiate and instruct; it is to be in the flesh of
man and in his heart. It is to expand, by means of
Israel, beyond Israel, till it is universal in its
effects; a chosen thing is to be its source; and all
families of the earth are to be exalted to the
same redemption. Last, at least in that single
passage, it is to be brought about by some kind of
substitution. "He was oppressed and he was
afflicted . . . for the transgression of my people
was he stricken." "For my thoughts are not your
thoughts, neither are your ways my ways, saith
the Lord."

Such is the prophetic movement towards the
recovery of that old simple knowledge of good as
good; such the promise to the righteous and

repentant. It is still a question how sin can be pardoned and in what manner and by what He it can be vicariously borne. But the Old Testament would not be the great book it is if it did not go further on the other side. There is a state of being which discovers, humanly speaking, the monotonous result of man's original choice. It might almost be said that Ecclesiastes represents a state of mind for which the prophets, with their minds set on righteousness, have not allowed. It is, in some sense, a classical expression of utter boredom, though the boredom is set to such high counterpoint that its very expression is exciting. No one who can enjoy Ecclesiastes can be as bored as Ecclesiastes. Indeed the word is too poor for the grand universality of the meaning. Yet it can hardly be called despair, for if it is despair, it is despair of a particular kind; more like that recorded by the poets at times.

> So much I feel my genial spirits droop,
> my hopes all flat, nature within me seems
> in all her functions weary of herself
>
> My genial spirits fail;
> and what can these [the outer world] avail
> To lift the smothering weight from off my
>   breast?

It is wan hope, the despair of life itself prolonged through the going-on of life itself, the core of the

fruit of the tree of knowledge of good and evil.
There is here no immorality; the prophets
themselves could hardly complain that Ecclesiastes
is hunting after any of the sins they so vehemently
denounce. It is possible to relate the book to
Solomon in his less moral periods, but that
would be to force our own biographical interpretation, like explaining Hamlet by the Earl of
Essex, and our own moral, in determining that
Ecclesiastes must be wicked because he is bored.
In fact Solomon, or (as it is safer to call him)
Ecclesiastes, is not aware of any particular sin.
On the contrary, he began by following wisdom,
and only when he found that wisdom brought him
heaviness of heart did he turn to other methods,
with the same result. He has sought out enjoyment and all the great occupations of kings—
building, planting, art—and all these labours are a
joy for a while, till they fail as wisdom failed. He
finds the same thing is true of righteousness
itself. The righteous have the reward of the
wicked; the wicked have the reward of the
righteous. Knowledge of good and knowledge of
evil come to the same thing in the end; the second
knowledge negatives all; "there is no profit under
the sun." And there is no other side to the sun;
two-dimensioned only, the flat light shines on a
flat world from which the third dimension of
significance has departed. That lack of significance is sometimes a pleasantness and a joy—
even a necessity if we are to enjoy significance at

other times, and God must sometimes deign to hide himself. But now it is continual, and therefore has lost all value. A single-toned universe is unbearable. "I said that this also is vanity." The too-famous refrain closes all activity, and the Canon of the Bible contains, by the peculiar inspiration of Providence, a complete rejection of life. "Therefore I hated life; because the work that is wrought under the sun is grievous unto me: for all is vanity and vexation of spirit." And again, more sublimely: "Whereupon I praised the dead which are already dead more than the living which are yet alive. Yea, better is he than both they, which hath not yet been, who hath not seen the evil work that is done under the sun." Death is release, for life is worse than death, and yet also death is worse than life. The living have one single advantage; they have a hope. "The living know that they shall die; but the dead know not anything." The paradox of vanity is complete, and the full force of it sinks slowly into the heart. This is the conclusion of the knowledge of good and evil. Life, in that first great myth of origin, was given as good, and man thought it would be fine and godlike to enjoy it also as evil. This is the result—life is no good and death is no good, and the most fortunate are those who have not been. For man's nature is such that he must prefer to live in hope of death than not to live or hope at all. The single joy of existence is to know that existence will stop; by so much, and by so much only, existence is better than non-existence. And then it does stop, and there is an end; "man cometh in with vanity, and departeth in darkness." Lucretius consoled men for death; "think—you will not then desire; you will not miss anything, for you will not know of anything to miss." That is no satisfaction here.

Along with this decision runs a willing acknowledgment of the existence of God, and of the will of God towards righteousness. Ecclesiastes does not object to righteousness; only the end of righteousness is like the end of everything else. God exists—certainly; man is to obey him—certainly. But life is unrelated to this obedience. His conclusion therefore is: "Remember thy Creator, and hope to die." He does not argue with God like Job. Job desires death, and curses his birth, but he vehemently demands that God shall explain the whole accursed business. The docility of Ecclesiastes does not argue or demand; the result of that too would doubtless be vanity. He accepts all, without delight, without anger, without goodwill. He has rejected life and death, and there is nothing to do but to put up with what comes. But Job had refused to put up with what came, until in the end the Lord himself came, compelled out of the air into the whirlwind of reply by the challenging voice of his creature.

It is true Ecclesiastes does not take immortality into account. The dead, to him, are wholly or entirely dead. But the mere introduction of

immortality will not help. There is no reason to
suppose that an experience of unending time
would be happier than an experience of a brief
period of time, unless something else were
introduced, and of the introduction of anything
else Ecclesiastes has seen no signs. On the
contrary, immortality, he thinks, leaves those
subject to it worse off by depriving them of their
one positive joy—the hope of death. No, "let us
hear the conclusion of the whole matter: Fear
God and keep his commandments, for this is the
whole duty of man. For God shall bring every
work into judgement, with every secret thing."
This, no doubt, is wisdom; and wisdom also is
vanity and vexation of spirit.

Such, beyond the prophets, is the undertone of
man's knowledge; such is the wise man's judgement. The mystics and the saints desire and
demand and promise; the storm of divine anger
and divine peace rages from the heavens; an
infinite riddle of substitution is sung to the heart
of the devout. But Ecclesiastes spoke of what he
knew, and of what many millions of others have
known after him.

CHAPTER IV

The Precursor and the Incarnation of the Kingdom

THE earliest of the Gospels is asserted to be that called "of Mark"; it is certainly the shortest. As Genesis had explained what was happening by what had happened, so do the Gospels. They purport to be a record of the cause of certain definite experiences. The time and place of that cause are definitely marked. It occurs in certain named towns of the Roman Empire, in a period from 4 B.C. to A.D. 30, from forty to seventy years after the death of Julius Cæsar, and from fifteen to fifty years after the death of Virgil. The administration of the Imperial Government organizes everything, and the events are plotted along the lines of that organization. The *pietas* of the early and mythical wanderers has become a supernational civilization. The documents of the New Testament are themselves composed in or directed to localities in that inter-related whole, and before it is well understood what the Church is, it is at least clear that it is universal. At the same time, history and contemporaneity again go together, the obverse and the reverse of the coins of the kingdom of heaven. Its missionaries declared a unity, as they do to-day, a unity no more divided by two

thousand years than by two seconds. We certainly
have to separate them in thought, because of the
needs of the mind, as we have sometimes to
divide form and content in poetry. But as the
poetry is in fact one and indivisible, so is the fact;
so even is the doctrine. The thing as it happens on
the earth and in the world, the thing as it happens
on the earth and in the soul, are two stresses on one
fact; say, on one Word. The fact is the thing that
is supposed to have appeared, and the Gospel of
Mark is the shortest account. The Gospels called
"of Matthew" and "of Luke" are longer and
fuller. The Gospel called "of John" comes
nearer to describing the unity of the new thing in
world and soul; it is the limit of the permissible
influence of contemporary Greek philosophy, and
the repulse of the impermissible. To observe
something of the distinction one has only to
consider the *Symposium* of Plato with the Gospel
of John, and remark the difference in their
attitude towards matter.

It is asserted that the Gospel according to Mark
was in circulation at Rome by the year 75. If so,
and if the Gospel of Mark represents at all what
the Church believed or tried to believe in the
year 75, then certainly by the year 75 the Church
at the centre of a highly developed society had
already thrown over any idea (if any such idea had
ever existed) of a figure only of brotherly love and
international peace; the moral teacher expanding
the old Jewish ideas of pardon and righteousness

into a fresh beauty, and teaching ethics in the ancient maxim of the Golden Rule. Possibly a figure of this kind might be extracted from St. John's Gospel, by leaving out rather more than half of St. John's Gospel. But with the Gospel of St. Mark the thing is impossible. To remove the apocalyptic is not to leave the ethical but to leave nothing at all.

It is, of course, arguable that the influence of St. Paul, who is often regarded as the villain of early Christianity (the Claudius of a *Hamlet* from which Hamlet has been removed), had already had its perfect work. Or, since there had not been very much time for St. Paul to do it, perhaps someone earlier, an Ur-Paul, or (documentarily) the fatal and fascinating Q which no man has seen at any time but the contents of which we so neatly know. The weakness, credulity, and folly of that early disciple, or of all the early disciples, may have altered the original truth of the vagrant provincial professor of ethical beauty into something more closely corresponding to their romantic needs. St. Mark may be dogmatically asserted to have been an intentional or unintentional liar. But at least we have to admit his lies for the purpose of explaining that they are lies. They are our only evidence for whatever it was he was lying about. And as he was not lying in a sub-prefecture of Thule, but right in the middle of the Empire, so he was not lying about events older than the dynasties of Egypt or the cities of Assyria, but about events done on a hill outside a city on a Roman highway under the rule of the Princeps Augustus and his successor Tiberius. They were (in one sense or the other—or both) historic lies.

Our contemporary pseudo-acquaintance with the Christian idea has misled us in another point. It is generally supposed that his lies (if lies) are simple and easy. It is only by reading St. Mark that one discovers they are by no means simple or easy. It is very difficult to make out what is supposed to be happening. His book begins with a declaration: "The beginning of the Gospel of Jesus Christ, the Son of God." What the Son of God may be he does not explain, preferring to follow it up with a quotation from the old prophets which slides into an account of a certain John who came as the precursor of this Divine Hero. He has in St. Mark no other business, and this (though highly wrought to a fine passion of declamation and heraldry) is so in St. John. But in St. Luke there is something more. It is recorded that certain groups came to the Precursor —the common people, the tax-collectors, the soldiers. All these ask him for some kind of direction on conduct. St. Matthew adds the ecclesiastical leaders, but the Precursor offered them no more than invective. He answers the rest with instructions which amount very nearly to a gospel of temporal justice. All men are to share their goods freely and equally. The revenue officers are to make no personal profit out of their business. The soldiers are not to make their duties an excuse for outrage or violence; they (again) are to make no personal gain beyond their government pay. Share everything; neither by fraud nor by force let yourself be unfair to anyone; be content with your own proper pay. It is true he does not raise the question of the restoration of the dispossessed by force of arms; he is speaking of immediate duties as between individual and individual. "He that has two coats let him give to him that hath none." He prolongs the concern of the prophets with social injustice, without their denunciation of the proud. That had been declared, as a duty of the Imperial government, by the great poet dead forty-five years before:

Pacisque imponere morem,
Parcere subiectis et debellare superbos:

"To impose the habit of peace, to be merciful to the down-trodden, and to overthrow the proud." There had been a similar note in the private song (again according to St. Luke) of the Mother of the coming Hero: "the rich he hath sent empty away."

At this moment the Divine Thing appears (it will be remembered that St. Matthew uses the neuter—"that holy *thing*"; students of the Gospel may be excused for sometimes following the example, if only to remind ourselves of what the

Evangelists actually said). In the rest of St. Mark's first chapter, the account of his coming is purely apocalyptic. Witness is borne out of heaven and on earth and from hell. He (since the masculine pronoun is also and more frequently used) begins his own activities. He calls disciples; he works miracles of healing; he controls spirits; he teaches with authority. What does he teach? what do the devils fear and the celestials declare and men wonder at? "The time is fulfilled, and the kingdom of God is at hand; repent ye and believe the gospel."

Yes, but what gospel? what kind of kingdom? The Precursor had said almost the same thing. In some expectation one turns the page . . . several pages. The works of healing continue swiftly, interspersed with the Divine Thing's comments on himself, and his reasons for existing. They are still not very clear. The old prophetic cry of "pardon" returns. He has power to forgive sins— does he mean forget? He calls himself the "Son of Man"; he is lord of ritual observances such as the keeping of the Sabbath; there exists some state of eternal sin and damnation. There is something— presumably the kingdom of heaven—which cannot be reconciled with old things; new, it must be fitted to the new.

Presently, in the parables, the description of the kingdom is continued. It is a state of being, but not a state of being without which one can get along very well. To lose it is to lose everything else. It

is intensely dangerous, and yet easily neglected.
It involves repentance and it involves "faith"—
whatever "faith" may be. It is concerned with
himself, for he attributes to himself the power and
the glory. He says: "I say unto thee, Arise";
"it is I; be not afraid." The Sermon on the
Mount is full of his own decisions, just as it ramps
with hell and destruction and hypocrites and
being cast into the fire and trodden under foot and
demands for perfection and for joy (not for
resignation or endurance or forgiveness, not even
a pseudo-joy) under intolerable treatment. Moses
in old days had momentarily taken the power and
the glory to himself, and had been shut out of the
temporal promise. But the present Hero does it
continuously, until (in the topmost note of that
exalted arrogance) humility itself is vaunted, and
the only virtue that cannot be aware of itself
without losing its nature is declared by the Divine
Thing to be its own nature: "I am meek and
lowly of heart." This in the voice that says to the
Syrophœnician woman when she begs help for
her daughter: "It is not meet to take the children's
bread, and to cast it unto the dogs." It is true her
request is granted, in answer to her retort, something in the same manner as the Lord spoke to
Job in answer to his.

About halfway through the book as we have it,
there is a change. Up to Chapter viii it is possible to
believe that, though the doctrine is anything but
clear, the experience of the disciples is not unique.

Figures are sometimes met who overwhelm, frighten, and delight those who come in contact with them; personality, and so forth—and what they say may easily sound obscure. But in Chapter viii there is a sudden concentration and even exposition. The Hero demands from his disciples a statement, not of their repentence or righteousness or belief in the I AM, which is what the old prophets clamoured for, but of their belief in himself, and he follows it up with a statement of his own. They say: "Thou art the Christ." No doubt when we have looked up annotated editions and Biblical dictionaries, we know what "the Christ" means. It is "the Anointed One." But at the moment, there, it is a kind of incantation, the invocation of a ritual, antique, and magical title. Even if we look up the other Gospels and make it read: "Thou art the Christ, the Son of the living God," it does not much help. However inspired St. Peter may have been, it seems unlikely that he comprehended in a flash the whole complex business of Christian theology. What is the Son of God? The apostles and the devils agree; that is something. But on what do they agree?

The Divine Thing approves the salutation. It proceeds to define its destiny. It declares it is to suffer greatly, to be rejected by all the centres of jurisdiction, to be seized and put to death, and after three days it is to rise again from the dead. Protests are abusively tossed aside. In all three

gospels this definition of its immediate future is
followed by a definition of its further nature and
future; "the Son of Man" is to be seen in the
"glory of his Father and with the holy angels,"
that is, in the swift and geometrical glory seen by
Isaiah and Ezekiel, the fire of the wheels and the
flash of the living creatures, the terrible crystal
and the prism of the covenant above, the pattern
of heaven declared in heaven. The formula of the
knowledge of this pattern on earth is disclosed; it
is the loss of life for the saving of life, "for my sake
and the gospel's." It is the denial of the self and
the lifting of the cross.

The denial of the self has come, as is natural, to
mean in general the making of the self thoroughly
uncomfortable. That (though it may be all that is
possible) leaves the self still strongly existing.
But the phrase is more intellectual than moral, or
rather it is only moral because it is intellectual; it
is a denial of the consciousness of the existence of
the self at all. What had been the self is to become
a single individual, neither less nor more than
others; as it were, one of the living creatures that
run about and compose the web of the glory.
"Do unto others as you would they should do
unto you." The contemplation demanded is not
personal, of the self and of others—even in order
that the self may be unselfish—but abstract and
impartial. The life of the self is to be lost that the
individual soul may be found, in the pattern of the
words of the Son of Man. The kingdom is

immediately at hand—"Verily I say unto you, That there be some of them that stand here, which shall not taste of death, till they have seen the kingdom of God come with power"; again the words are historic and contemporary at once.

The declaration of the formula is followed by what is called the Transfiguration. Secluded among a few of his followers, the Divine Thing exhibits itself in a sudden brightness, in which, as if it receded into the eternal state of contemporaneousness, the ancient leaders of what had once been the inclusive-exclusive covenant of salvation are discerned to exchange speech with the new exclusive figure of inclusive beatitude. It is a vision which is to be kept a secret till the rising from the dead has been accomplished. But at least the kingdom has now been, to some extent, exhibited. Repentance is a preliminary to the denial of the self and the loss of the life, and the loss of the life for the saving of the life depends on that choosing of necessity by the Son of Man which will take him to his death and rising. "He set his face to go up to Jerusalem."

It is at some time during this period of the operation of the Christ that the problem of the Precursor reappears. Messengers from John arrive; "art thou he that was to come?" After they have been dismissed, the Christ, turning to those that stood by (as it were to his mother and to his brethren), makes the astonishing declaration that "among men born of women is none greater than

John the Baptist, yet the least in the Kingdom of Heaven is greater than he." The Church since then has implied that this can hardly be true in its literal sense, for the Precursor has been canonized (as it were, by acclamation) and been given a Feast to himself, a Primary Double of the First Class. Even so, even assuming that as a matter of fact the Precursor was and is one of the greatest in the kingdom of heaven, still the Christ must have had something in his mind. What, apart from the expectation of the Redeemer, was the gospel of the Precursor? It was something like complete equality and temporal justice, regarded as the duty of those who expect the kingdom. What has happened to that duty in the gospel of the Kingdom?

The new gospel does not care much about it. All John's doctrine is less than the least in the Kingdom. It cannot be bothered with telling people not to defraud and not to be violent and to share their superfluities. It tosses all that sort of thing on one side. Let the man who has two coats (said the Precursor) give one to the man who has none. But what if the man who has none, or for that matter the man who has three, wants to take one from the man who has two—what then? Grace of heaven! why, give him both. If a man has stolen the pearl bracelet, why, point out to him that he has missed the diamond necklace? Be content with your wages, said the Precursor. The Holy Thing decorated that advice with a suggestion that it is iniquity to be displeased when others who have done about a tenth as much work are paid as much money: "is thine eye evil because mine is good?" It is true that there is a reason—those who came in late had not been hired early. No one would accept that as a reason today—neither economist nor employer nor worker. But there is always a reason; the intellectual logic of the Prophets is carried on into the New Testament. Yet the separate and suitable reasons never quite account for the identical and indivisible command. The "sweet reasonableness" of Christ is always there, but it is always in a dance and its dancing hall is from the topless heavens to the bottomless abyss. Its balance is wholly in itself; it is philosophical and unconditioned by temporalities—"had, having, and in quest to have, extreme."

Half a hundred brief comments, flung out to the mob of men's hearts, make it impossible for a child of the kingdom, for a Christian, to talk of justice or injustice so far as he personally is concerned; they make it impossible for him to *complain* of the unfairness of anything. They do not, presumably, stop him noticing what has happened, but it can never be a matter of protest. Judgment and measurement are always discouraged. You may have them if you will, but there is a sinister note in the promise that they shall be measured back to you in the same manner: "good measure, pressed down and

running over shall men give into your bosoms."
If you must have law, have it, "till thou hast paid
the uttermost farthing."

What then of all the great tradition, the freeing
of slaves at the Exodus, the determination of the
prophets, the long effort against the monstrous
impiety of Cain? The answer is obvious; all that
is assumed as a mere preliminary. The rich, while
they remain rich, are practically incapable of
salvation, at which all the Apostles were exceedingly astonished. Their astonishment is
exceedingly funny to our vicariously generous
minds. But if riches are not supposed to be
confined to money, the astonishment becomes
more general. There are many who feel that while
God might damn Rothschild he could hardly
damn Rembrandt. Are the riches of Catullus and
Carnegie so unequal, though so different? Sooner
or later, nearly everyone is surprised at some kind
of rich man being damned. The Divine Thing,
for once, was tender to us; he restored a faint
hope: "with God all things are possible." But the
preliminary step is always assumed: "sell all that
thou hast and give it to the poor"—and then we
will talk. Then we will talk of that other thing
without which even giving to the poor is useless,
the thing for which at another time the precious
ointment was reserved from the poor, the thing
that is necessary to correct and qualify even good
deeds, the thing that is formulated in the words
"for my sake and the gospel's" or "in my name."

Good deeds are not enough; even love is not enough unless it is love of a particular kind. Long afterwards St. Paul caught up the dreadful cry: "though I bestow all my goods to feed the poor . . . and have not charity, it profiteth me nothing." It is not surprising that Messias saw the possibility of an infinitely greater knowledge of evil existing through him than had been before: "blessed is he whosoever shall not be offended at me."

The Incarnation of the Kingdom has declared its destiny, the formula by which man may be unified with it, the preliminaries necessary to the spiritual initiation. The records of the Synoptics proceed to the awful and familiar tale: to the entry of the Divine Thing into Jerusalem, to its making of itself a substance of communication through the flesh, to its Passion. "The Son of Man is betrayed into the hands of sinners." In the ancient myth something of that kind had happened to the good, the good in which the Adam had lived. But that good had not, in the myth, been imagined as a consciousness. The kingdom of heaven then had not been shown as affected by the sin of the Adam; only the Adam. The patience which had been proclaimed in the covenants had been the self-restraint of the Creator, but not—there—of the Victim. Another side of the æonian process has issued slowly into knowledge; the operation of that in the Adam and in their descendants which had remained everlastingly related to the good.

The Gospel called "of John" begins with that
original. The Divine Thing is there identified
with the knowledge of good which indefectibly
exists in every man—indefectibly even though it
should be experienced only as hell—"the light
which lighteth every man." It is also that by
which communication with the heaven of perfection is maintained, "ascending and descending." But this state of being which is called "the
kingdom of heaven" in the Synoptics is called in
St. John "eternal life." There is no space here to
work out singly the various definitions of itself
which it provides in this Gospel. Briefly, it
declares itself to be the union of heaven and earth
(i. 51); the one absolutely necessary thing for
escape from a state in which the contradiction of
good is preferred (iii, 16, 36); it is the perfect
satisfaction of desire (vi, 35; x, 27–8); it is judgment (v, 25–30; xii, 46–8); it is in perfect union
with its Origin (x, 30; xiv, 11); it is universal and
inclusive (xv. 5; xvii. 21); it restores the truth
(v. 33; vii. 31–2; xviii. 37). Of these the last is
perhaps the most related to the present argument.
For by truth must be meant at least perfect
knowledge (within the proper requisite degrees).
"Ye shall know the truth, and the truth shall
make you free." Right knowledge and freedom
are to be one.

It is this "truth" of which the Divine Hero
speaks at the time of the Passion which he had
prophesied—as necessity and as his free choice.

Before one of the jurisdictions by which he is rejected and condemned he declares: "To this end was I born, and for this cause came I into the world, that I should bear witness unto the truth. Everyone that is of the truth heareth my voice." He formally claimed before another the ritual titles of Son of God and Son of Man, and his future descent "in the clouds of heaven" and in the glory of heaven. But before then the earlier proclamation, "the kingdom of heaven is at hand," has changed. It has become concentrated; if the kingdom, then the moment of the arrival of the kingdom. The Gospels break into peremptory phrases: "My time is at hand," "this night," "this hour;" an image of the hour absorbed into the Holy Thing is thrown up—"this cup;" the hour arrives—"behold, the Son of Man is betrayed into the hands of sinners."

Around that moment the world of order and judgment, of Virgil and the Precursor, of Pharaoh and Cain, rushes up also. Its good and its evil are both concerned, for it cannot very well do other than it does do. The knowledge of good as evil has made the whole good evil to it; it has to reject the good in order to follow all that it can understand as good. When Caiaphas said that "it was good that one man should die for the people," he laid down a principle which every government supports and must support. Nor, though Christ has denounced the government for its other sins, does he denounce either Caiaphas or Pilate for his

own death. He answers the priest; he condescends
to discussion with the Roman. Only to Herod he
says nothing, for Herod desired neither the
ecclesiastical nor the political good; he wanted
only miracles to amuse him. The miracles of
Christ are accidental, however efficient; the
kingdom of heaven fulfils all earthly laws because
that is its nature but it is concerned only with its
own, and to try to use it for earth is to lose heaven
and gain nothing for earth. It may be taken by
violence but it cannot be compelled by violence;
its Incarnation commanded that he should be
awaited everywhere but his effectiveness demanded nowhere. Everything must be made
ready and then he will do what he likes. This
maxim, which is the condition of all prayer, has
involved the Church in a metaphysic of prayer
equivalent to "Heads, I win; tails, you lose."

The three jurisdictions acted according to all
they could understand of good: Caiaphas upon all
he could know of the religious law, Pilate of the
Virgilian equity, Herod of personal desire. The
Messias answered them in that first word of the
Cross which entreated pardon for them precisely
on the ground of their ignorance: "forgive them,
for they know not what they do." The knowledge
of good and evil which man had desired is offered
as the excuse for their false knowledge of good.
But the offer brings their false knowledge into
consciousness, and will no longer like the prophets
blot it out. The new way of pardon is to be

different from the old, for the evil is still to be
known. It is known, in what follows, by the
Thing that has come down from Heaven. He
experiences a complete and utter deprivation of
all knowledge of the good. The Church has never
defined the Atonement. It has contented itself
with saying that the Person of the kingdom there
assumed into itself the utmost possible capacities
of its own destruction and they could not destroy
it. It separated itself from all good deliberately
and (as it were) superfluously: "thinkest thou I
cannot now pray to the Father and he shall
presently give me more than twelve legions of
angels? But how then shall the scriptures be
fulfilled, that thus it must be?" It could, it seems,
still guiltlessly free itself, but it has made its own
promise and will keep it. Its impotency is
deliberate. It denies its self; it loses its life to save
it; it saves others because it cannot, by its decisions,
save itself. It remains still exclusive and inclusive; it excludes all consent to the knowledge of
evil, but it includes the whole knowledge of evil
without its own consent. It is "made sin," in St.
Paul's phrase. The prophecy quoted concerning
this paradox of redemption is "A bone of him shall
not be broken," and this is fulfilled; as if the frame
of the universe remains entire, but its life is
drawn out of it, as if the pattern of the glory
remained exact but the glory itself were drawn
away. The height of the process begins with the
Agony in the Garden, which is often quoted for

our encouragement; he shuddered and shrank. The shrinking is part of the necessity; he "must" lose power; he "must" know fear. He "must" be like the Adam in the garden of the myth, only where they fled from their fear into the trees he goes among the trees to find his fear; he is secluded into terror. The process reaches its height, after from the cross he has still asserted the *pietas*, the exchanged human responsibility, of men: "behold thy son, behold thy mother," and after he has still declared the pure dogma of his nature, known now as hardly more than dogma: "today thou shalt be with me in Paradise." This is what he has chosen, and as his power leaves him he still chooses, to believe. He becomes, but for that belief, a state wholly abandoned.

Gibbon, in that superb as well as solemn sneer which is one of the classic pages of English prose as well as one of the supreme attacks on the whole history, may have been right. The whole earth may not have been darkened, nor even the whole land. Pliny and Seneca may have recorded no wonder because there was no wonder to record. The sun may have seemed to shine on Calvary as on many another more protracted agony. Or there may have been a local eclipse, or whatever other phenomenon the romantic pietists can invent to reconcile themselves to the other side. But that the life of the whole of mankind began to fail in that hour is not incredible; that the sun and all light, without as within, darkened before men's eyes, that the swoon of something more than death touched them, and its sweat stood on their foreheads to the farthest ends of the world. The Thing that was, and had always been, and must always be; the fundamental humanity of all men; the Thing that was man rather than a man, though certainly incarnated into the physical appearance of a man; the Thing that was Christ Jesus, knew all things in the deprivation of all goodness.

The darkness passed; men went on their affairs. He said: "It is finished." The Passion and the Resurrection have been necessarily divided in ritual and we think of them as separate events. So certainly they were, and yet not as separate as all that. They are two operations in one; they are the hour of the coming of the kingdom. A new knowledge arises. Men had determined to know good as evil; there could be but one perfect remedy for that—to know the evil of the past itself as good, and to be free from the necessity of the knowledge of evil in the future; to find right knowledge and perfect freedom together; to know all things as occasions of love. The Adam and their children had been involved in a state of contradiction within themselves. The law had done its best by imposing on that chaos of contradiction a kind of order, by at least calling definite things good and definite things evil. The prophets had urged this method: repent, "cease to do evil, learn to do well." But even allowing that, in all times and places, it was possible to know what was good and what was evil, was it as easy as all that? Or what of Job who had done well and was overthrown? Or Ecclesiastes who had sought out righteousness and found it was all much the same vanity in the end? How could the single knowledge be restored? Or if the myth itself were false, how could the single knowledge be gained— the knowledge of perfection in all experience which man naturally desires and naturally believes, and as naturally denies and contradicts?

The writings of the early masters of the new life, the life that was declared after the Resurrection, are full of an awful simplicity. The thing has happened; the kingdom is here. "Fear not, little flock," wrote one of them, "it is your Father's good pleasure to give you the kingdom." "What shall deliver me," wrote another, "from the body of this death? I thank God, through Jesus Christ our Lord." This clarity of knowledge rides through the Epistles. All is most well; evil is "pardoned"—it is known after another manner; in an interchange of love, as a means of love, there-fore as a means of the good. *O felix culpa*—pardon is no longer an oblivion but an increased knowledge, a knowledge of all things in a perfection of joy.

It is the name now given to the heavenly knowledge of the evil of earth; evil is known as an occasion of good, that is, of love. It has been always so known on the side of heaven, but now

it can be so known on the side of earth also.
Pardon, or reconciliation, was not defined by the
prophets as more than oblivion, for in time mankind had not experienced that reconciliation. Nor
could mankind, by itself, ever reach it, for mankind by itself could not endure the results of its
choice, the total deprivation of good, and yet
recover joyous awareness of good. What mankind
could not do, manhood did, and a manhood which
was at the disposal of all men and women. It was
therefore possible now for mankind itself to know
evil as an occasion of heavenly love. It was not
inappropriate that the condition of such a pardon
should be repentance, for repentance is no more
than a passionate intention to know all things after
the mode of heaven, and it is impossible to know
evil as good if you insist on knowing it as evil.
Pardon, as between any two beings, is a re-
identification of love, and it is known so in the
most tender and the most happy human relationships. But there is a profound difference between
any such re-identification of love between heaven
and earth and between earth and earth. What
may be justly required in the one case must not
be required in the other. It is all very well for the
Divine Thing of heaven to require some kind of
intention of good, not exactly as a condition of
pardon but as a means of the existence of its
perfection. Men were never meant to be as gods
or to know as gods, and for men to make any such
intention a part of their pardon is precisely to try

to behave as gods. It is the renewal of the first
and most dreadful error, the desire to know as
gods; the reversal of the Incarnation, by which
God knew as Man, the heresy of thought and
action denounced in the Athanasian Creed—it is
precisely the attempt to convert the Godhead into
flesh and not the taking of the manhood into God.
The intention to do differently may be passionately
offered; it must never be required—not in the
most secret recesses of that self which can only
blush with shame to find itself pardoning and with
delight at the infinite laughter of the universe at a
created being forgiving another created being. The
ancient cry of "Don't do it again" is never a part
of pardon. It is conceivable that St. Peter re-
identified love between hinself and his brother
four hundred and ninety times in a day; it is
inconceivable that each time he made it a condition of love that it shouldn't happen again,—it
would be a slur on intelligence as well as love. To
consent to know evil as good only on condition
that the evil never happens again is silly; it is
conditioning one's knowledge—as if one con-
sented to know that the Antipodes existed only
on condition that no one ever mentioned the
Antipodes. All limitation of pardon must come,
if at all, from the side of the sinner, in the frequent
cry of "I won't do it again", in the more frequent
cry of "I won't, but I shall . . ." Heaven has
had to explain to us not only itself but ourselves;
it has had to create for us not only pardon but the

nature of the desire for pardon. It has therefore defined the cry of the sinner, but it has not suggested that other sinners should take upon themselves to demand the cry before they submit, with their brothers, to its single glorious existence in both.

He rose; he manifested; he talked of "the things pertaining to the kingdom." He exhibited the actuality of his body, carrying the lovely and adorable matter, with which all souls were ever-lastingly conjoined, into his eternity. He left one great commandment—satisfy hunger: "feed the lambs", "feed the sheep". Beyond the Petrine law he cast the Johannine—"if I will that he tarry till I come . . ." but the coming may be from moment to moment and the tarrying from moment to moment. "Jesus said not unto him, He shall not die; but, If I will that he tarry till I come, what is that to thee?" It is as if, from moment to moment, he withdrew and returned, swifter than lightning, known in one mode and another mode and always new. The new life might still be sequential (in the order of time) but every instant was united to the Origin, and complete and absolute in itself. "Behold, I come quickly" —the coming and the going one, the going and the coming one, and all is joy. "It is not for you to know the times and the seasons . . . but you shall be witnesses to me . . . to the uttermost ends of the earth," through all the distances and all the operations of holy matter.

Then, as if it withdrew into the air within the air, and the air became a cloud about its passage, scattering promises of power, the Divine Thing parted and passed.

CHAPTER V

The Theology of Romantic Love

"THERE are," wrote Wordsworth,

> There are in our existence spots of time,
> That with distinct pre-eminence retain
> A renovating virtue, whence, depressed
> By false opinion and contentious thought,
> Or aught of heavier or more deadly weight,
> In trivial occupations, and the round
> Of ordinary intercourse, our minds
> Are nourished and invisibly repaired.

It is these pre-eminent and renovating moments which differ in different civilizations and philosophies. Life itself is much of a muchness wherever it is lived, but our efforts to draw the muchness (in the Dormouse's phrase) change. It may not make much difference, as that other great creature, Dr. Johnson, who had so much in common with the figures of Alice's Wonderland, told Boswell, under what government a man lives. But the kind of philosophy under which he lives does make a little, by means of the pre-eminent moments. Those moments are often interpreted in terms of the then dominant philosophy, but they retain their richness, and (at least for awhile)

83

they enrich the philosophy. An exchange takes place between ideas and events, and that exchange is communicated, at those moments, first to the more creative and afterwards to all minds.

In the centuries after the passing of Christ there grew up in Europe a great metaphysical civilization, a society as much based on a philosophical principle as the first Roman Empire had been on the evasion of philosophical principles. The fundamental idea was salvation. The grand substitution had been, and was being, carried out, and society was to be organized on the basis of a belief in substitution and salvation. It had of course many other elements; it had something of the Precursor, and a very great deal of Pharaoh, but it thought in terms of the Apostles. The celebration of the Mass did not so much prolong the Sacrifice in time as turn time back to the Sacrifice; communion mystically united the pious to heaven and the impious to hell; the ceremony of penance was instituted to spread everywhere the public news of a secret pardon. To the naturally outstanding figures of kings, conquerors, lawgivers, and even poets, were now added the supernaturally outstanding figures of those who, by a passion of courtesy towards God and man, seemed even on earth to have fully lost their own lives and attained some other. Experience underwent new interpretation. The Revolution, which had been assumed by Christ as a preliminary to the Kingdom, became entangled with the principles of the Church, and has (to the irritation of both groups of minds) remained somewhat entangled. The Revolution may exist without any demand for the Church, but the Church has never existed long anywhere without creating a demand for a Revolution. "The poor ye have always with you," said Christ, and wherever his tradition has gone we have been made acutely aware of them. The idea of social justice became important. The idea of tragedy lost its importance—almost its nature. In this world all was, in the end, under Providence, however detestable the enemies of Providence; as when, in one of his loveliest passages, Dante speaks of Luck as being one of the primal creatures, who for ever enjoys her own beatitude, while fools blaspheme her below. Nor could the other world be tragic, since there could hardly be tragedy, whatever grief, in a man's obstinate determination to be damned. So Death at once gained and lost; it gained in frightfulness and in beauty; it lost the profound solace of Lucretius, for immortality (whether a boon or a curse) was now a fact, and final oblivion was forbidden to comfort man's mind. All these alterations filled men's pre-eminent moments with new nourishment and new repair. The imagination of the world and of heaven had changed.

Of all these alterations one affected perhaps more than all the rest (except for the central dogmas) the casual fancies and ordinary outlook of men and women. As a historic fact the change

has been described in words better than any I
could find by Mr. C. S. Lewis, in one of the most
important critical books of our time, *The Allegory
of Love*. I may therefore quote him at some
length:

   " . . . It seems to us natural that love should
   be the commonest theme of serious imaginative
   literature: but a glance at classical antiquity or
   at the Dark Ages at once shows us that what we
   took for 'nature' is really a special state of
   affairs, which will probably have an end, and
   which certainly had a beginning in eleventh-
   century Provence. It seems—or it seemed to us
   till lately—a natural thing that love (under
   certain conditions) should be regarded as a
   noble and ennobling passion: it is only if we
   imagine ourselves trying to explain this doctrine
   to Aristotle, Virgil, St. Paul, or the author of
   Beowulf, that we become aware how far from
   natural it is."

   " . . . French poets, in the eleventh century,
   discovered or invented, or were the first to
   express, that romantic species of passion which
   English poets were still writing about in the
   nineteenth. They effected a change which
   has left no corner of our ethics, our imagination, or our daily life untouched, and they
   erected impassable barriers between us and
   the classical past or the Oriental present.
   Compared with this revolution the Renaissance

is a mere ripple on the surface of literature."

" . . . The new thing itself I do not pretend
to explain. Real changes in human sentiment
are very rare—there are perhaps three or four
on record—but I believe that they occur, and
that this is one of them."

There entered into the relations between the
sexes a philosophical, even a religious, idea.[1]
That idea had a very long life before it, and was
to undergo many unfortunate and fortunate
chances. On the one hand, like many other
religious ideas, it was to become a superstition;
on the other hand, it was to be, naturally but
regrettably, cold-shouldered by the ecclesiastical
authorities. It was to be an indulgence to the
populace and a stumbling-block to the Puritans—
using both words of intellectual states of mind.
It was to save and endanger souls. And it is still
quite uncertain what will happen to it. It may
utterly disappear from the earth. But if not, the
popular idea of it will probably have to undergo
a good deal of purification. In fact, and in itself,
it is a thing not of superstition and indulgence,
but of doctrine and duty, and not of achievement
but of promise.

The pre-eminent moment of romantic love is
not, of course, confined to the moment of

[1] I am aware that in the Middle Ages this idea involved
conventionally certain conditions, but since they are not of
its intellectual essence they need not be here considered.

romantic sex love. There are other moments of
intense experience combined with potentiality of
further experience. Great art has it and politics
and nature and (it is said) maturity. But few of
these have had the same universality and few,
owing to the chance of genius, have undergone
the same analysis. Wordsworth began the task
of the analysis of man's experience of nature as a
precursor and means to something greater, but
for various reasons he left it unfinished. Nature,
until recently, had become as much of a superstition as romantic love; it looks, however, as if it
would have a shorter period of influence.

The difficulty in any discussion of such
experiences is in the finding common ground for
discussion. There is no accepted agreement upon
what the state which our grandfathers used to call
"falling in love" involves. It is neither sex
appetite pure and simple; nor, on the other hand,
is it necessarily related to marriage. It is something like a state of adoration, and it has been
expressed, of course, by the poets better than
by anyone else. Perhaps therefore the most
convenient way of defining it will be to take a
quotation from one of them, and that not from
any of the more extreme Romantics but from
Milton (who has long enough been regarded as
both pious and puritanical). It has here the
additional advantage of being imagined as spoken
by Adam of Eve, and therefore as an imagined
expression of that state of the good in which,

before the Fall, they existed. It comes from
Paradise Lost, Book viii. 546–59:

> " . . . when I approach
> Her loveliness, so absolute she seems
> And in herself complete, so well to know
> Her own, that what she wills to do or say
> Seems wisest, virtuousest, discreetest, best.
> All higher knowledge in her presence falls
> Degraded; Wisdom in discourse with her
> Loses, discount'nanced, and like Folly shows;
> Authority and Reason on her wait,
> As one intended first, not after made
> Occasionally; and, to consummate all,
> Greatness of mind and nobleness their seat
> Build in her loveliest, and create an awe
> About her, as a guard angelic placed."

This then is the contemplation of the object of
love from a state of romantic love. There has been
and is, now as always, only one question about
this state of things: is it serious? is it capable of
intellectual treatment? is it capable of belief,
labour, fruition? is it (in some sense or other)
true? It is, of course, true to Adam if the vision
has so appeared to him. It was certainly a vision,
to Adam, and in the poem, of something like the
kingdom of heaven on earth; Eve is at once an
inhabitant of the kingdom and the means by
which the kingdom is seen. Can this state of
things be treated as the first matter of a great
experiment? and if so, what exactly is the

material? and what exactly are the best conditions of the experiment? The end, of course, is known by definition of the kingdom: it is the establishment of a state of *caritas*, of pure love, the mode of expansion of one moment into eternity. It is, in fact, another example of the operation of the inclusive-exclusive thing; only in this case it is Adam, in the poem, and we, outside the poem, who are expected to do something about it.

There was, in the history of Christendom, a genius of the greatest power whose imagination worked on this theme, and that was Dante. The range of his whole work provides a complete account of the making of the experiment and of its success. It is not, of course, the only theme in Dante: *tot homini quot Dantes*. But at least it is one, and it happens to be one which he very consciously asserted. We shall not therefore be ingeniously extracting a gospel from him of which he knew nothing if we believe him. (There used certainly to be some critics who maintained that there never was a girl in Dante's life at all; at least, any denial of Beatrice must mean this or it means nothing. Once let any girl in—including Gemma Donati—and the principle has been admitted, and only the details can be discussed.) It is not possible here to make any effort to trace the whole philosophical journey. All that can be done is to take, because it is done so much better than we can do it, an analysis here and there.

The journey begins in the *New Life* with the first meeting with Beatrice at the age of nine, and with the second meeting at the age of eighteen. It proceeds through every kind of concern until it ends, at almost the close of the *Comedy*, with a state in which those first Beatrician encounters, which were once full of such a thrilling *tremendum*, seem almost paltry, except that they were the beginning of all, compared to the massive whole of single and exchanged Love. In reaching the end, we reach (as in all poetry) the beginning also; the *New Life*, like the *Hell* and the *Purgatory*, exists only by, in, and for the *Paradise* that includes them.

The description of the Beatrician encounters is in the *New Life*. A more intellectual and analytical definition is in the *Banquet*. It is true that it there occurs because of another lady, the "Lady of the Window", but that does not alter the definitions. The great love poets may have been monogamic in the sense of having one lady at a time; it cannot be said that they had one lady all the time. Nor indeed can it very easily be maintained that Dante was a striking example of New Testament monogamy, considering the extent to which his imagination concentrated itself on one woman while he was married to another. It is part of the incredible irony of the kingdom of heaven that it should produce the most stupendous and scientific statement of the experiment from a poet whom the stricter moralists of the experiment are compelled to disavow or to disguise.

The experience of romantic love then is described in the *New Life* and analyzed in the *Banquet.* The intellect is always called on to do its part. The appearance of Beatrice and her image is of so noble a virtue that "at no time it suffered Love to rule over me without the faithful council of Reason in things where such council was useful". The first appearance of Beatrice produces three separate effects: it moves the heart as the seat of spiritual emotions, the brain as the centre of perception, and the liver as the place of corporal emotions. It is much to be wished that English literature had kept liver as well as heart; we have to use one word for both emotional states —what (reverting to the old ambiguity of heaven) we might call the spiritual and the spatial heaven of romantic love. Dante did his part in describing the spatial heavens, but it is the spiritual which are here the concern. The following points may be briefly noted (they are taken from sections 3–8 of the third Treatise of the *Convivo;* the translation is from W. W. Jackson's version published by the Clarendon Press).

(1). The intellect "in discoursing of her, many times wished to infer things about her, though I could not understand them." The experience— the sight, that is, of the beloved—arouses a sense of intense significance, a sense that an explanation of the whole universe is being offered, and indeed in some sense understood; only it cannot yet be defined. Even when the intellect seems to apprehend, it cannot express its purpose; "the tongue cannot follow that which the intellect sees".

(2). "She is . . . the pattern of man's essence existing in thought within the divine mind . . . she is as completely perfect as the essence of man can possibly be." She is, that is, the perfect centre and norm of humanity; others exist, it seems, because and in so far as, they resemble her virtue. The extraordinary vision is that of the ordinary thing *in excelsis*.

(3). " . . . The experiences which may be had of her in these operations which are peculiar to the rational soul, into which the divine light radiates with less hindrance, I mean in speech and in the acts which may be called behaviour and carriage." It is a convention of love-poetry to speak of light emanating from the person of the beloved; the dichotomy of metaphysics is between those who believe that it does and those who do not. This does not seem to be arguable. The forehead and the hand are radiant; she dissemi-nates glory. Or they do not, and she does not; if it seems so, it does but seem. But no lover was ever content to allow that it was but a seeming; rather, it is to be that portion of the divine light which, in the eternal creation of her in heaven, possesses her. "The light that lightens every man that comes into the world" is made visible through her, by the will of grace, and by that alone. It seems that no one yet discovered that light of

glory in any woman or any man by hunting for it;
it seems that it may exist where it is not wanted.
It has its own methods; "my ways are not your
ways, saith the Lord." It is not of a nature
certainly to rival the electric light, but whether
that is due to its weakness or to the lover's
imperfection is another matter. The schools are
divided.

(4). "This lady is a thing visibly miraculous,
of which the eyes of men may daily have experience, and this marvel makes all others possible
in our eyes . . . this lady with her wondrous
aspect assists our faith. Therefore was she from
eternity so ordained". By "faith" there Dante
means faith in "Him who was crucified"—but
then to Dante He who was crucified was a thing
natural and fundamental, and not odd and all
religious. It is perhaps rather the word "eternity"
which is here suggestive. She appears with this
quality, as of something unaffected by time; it is
the metaphysical association of the visible light.
She is the substance of spirit.

(5). "I affirm, therefore, that, since we have
now ascertained the meaning of this section in
which this lady is extolled with regard to her soul,
one must now go on to perceive how . . . I extol
her with regard to her body. And I say that in
her aspect things appear which reveal 'some of
the joys' (among the many other joys) of Paradise.
The noblest pleasure . . . is to feel content, and
this is the same as to be blest; and this pleasure,

although in a different way, is truly found in the aspect of this lady . . . with much pleasure does her beauty feed the eyes of those who behold her. But this contentment is different in kind from that felt in Paradise, which is everlasting; for this everlasting contentment cannot fall to anyone here." The two places where the beauty of the soul most chiefly appears are the eyes and the mouth, and it is the integrity and modesty of the lady that are there mostly to be admired; one may say, the right proportion of candour and restraint, the perfect balance of virtue, opposed yet co-existent.

(6). Her beauty "surpasses our intellect" "as the sun surpasses weak sight, not indeed that which is healthy and strong." The weak sight of the mind cannot properly contemplate this beauty, for "after gazing freely on it, the soul becomes intoxicated, so that she goes astray in all her operations." This saying is reminiscent of Messias: "blessed is he whosoever shall not be offended at me", to whom I am not a cause of greater evil. The glory is apt to dazzle the beholder unless he already has a mind disposed to examine the pattern of the glory. It is more important to do the work of the kingdom than to say "Lord, Lord". Indeed, it is by some such going astray that the theology of Romantic Love has been neglected in favour of the superstitions and fables. The effort after the pattern marks the difference. The superstitions make heaven and

earth in the form of the beloved; the theology
declares that the beloved is the first preparatory
form of heaven and earth. Its controlling maxim
is that these things are first seen through Beatrice
as a means; the corollary is that they are found
through Beatrice as a first means only. The
preposition refers not only to sight but to progress.
For

(7). "Her beauty has power to renovate nature
in those who behold her, which is a marvellous
thing. And this confirms what has been said . . .
that she is the helper of our faith". This is perhaps
the most profound, most universal, and most
widely confirmed saying of all. It is the Dantean
equivalent of all the resolutions and reformations
rashly attributed to the influence of the beloved.
It is also the Dantean equivalent of the first coming
of the kingdom. He says, soon after: "She was
created not only to make a good thing better, but
also to turn a bad thing into good." Things
intolerable outside a state of love become blessed
within: laughter and love convert for a moment
the dark habitations within the soul to renewed
gardens in Eden. The primal knowledge is
restored, and something like pardon restores
something like innocence. The "new life" exists.
It cannot continue to exist permanently without
faith and labour. Nothing that comes down from
heaven can. But it renews nature if only for
a moment; it flashes for a moment into the lover
the life he was meant to possess instead of his

own by the exposition in her of the life she was meant to possess instead of her own. They are "in love".

(8). "This is she who maketh humble all the self-willed; she was the thought of him who set the universe in motion." She is the phenomenon of the centre; and the chief grace she bestows is humility—the self-forgetfulness which (only) makes room for adoration. She is the vision of the divine glory and the means of the divine grace, and she herself is irresponsible for it and almost irrelevant to it. She is the Mother of Love—of *caritas*, and even of a *caritas* beyond any *caritas* we can imagine; she is the chosen Mother of the goodwill of God.

These then are certain of the definitions which Dante gives of the effect of the appearance of Beatrice. It must be left to any reader to decide how far they form—at least partially—a correct account of a young man in the state of having "fallen in love". *Mutatis mutandis*, they may apply to the woman; though, since she is not in Dante, it is rather to Milton's Eve that we must go for a description of her. It is a not unpleasant thought that the word Fall occurs in this experience also; as if the divine grace, after man had insisted on falling once into a divided and contradictory knowledge, had arranged itself to trick him into an unexpected fall into restored and single knowledge. The inclusive-exclusive is a marked sign here of the means of salvation. Eve, Beatrice, or whoever, is certainly her peculiar and (in vision) indefectible self. But she is also the ordinary girl exalted into this extraordinary; she is the norm of all ladies, even if the others do not seem (in the lover's vision) to reach it. The union of flesh and spirit, visible in her (or him), is credible everywhere; indeed, that union, which so much poetry has desired to describe, is understood as more profound and more natural than the dichotomy, of experience or of expression, which has separated them. She is inclusive of both, and exclusive of their separateness. She is, in a final paradox, inclusive even of moments when she is none of these things, and the grace of that state is not least revealed when it excludes itself, as it were, and includes a happy and temporary ignorance of glory in favour of contented play.

The *New Life* had already personified the definitions of the *Banquet*. In the earlier book Beatrice is presented as having on Dante the effect which the *Banquet* analyzes. She exists (actual or not, but preferably, on the mere evidence, actual) as a form incarnating what is only afterwards understood as "the idea or abstraction of its kind". She meets him, and he her, in the activities of the city; ordinary things happen, and two extra-ordinary—for she snubs him, and she dies. Two or three incidents bear on the idea of her relation to God. The first is the moment when the girl comes down the street and says "Good morning" in passing. This thrilling and universal moment is known as "the salutation of Beatrice". So, of course, it is, and it is as serious (but not as artistic) as that. It is the flash of the moment in a word. Dante says: "I say that when she appeared from any place, there was through my hope of her admirable salutation, no enemy remaining to me, but a flame of *caritas* possessed me, which made me pardon anyone who had offended me; and if anyone had then asked me concerning anything, my answer would have been only *Love*, with a face clothed in humility." Or more colloquially: "I say that when she came along, I was so thrilled with the mere hope that she would notice me that I was friends with everyone, and utterly full of goodwill, and I was ready to forgive anyone who had offended me. If I had been asked any question at all I should have answered quite humbly *Love*". The pardon is not a cold superior thing but inevitably produced by *una fiamma di caritade*, a leaping momentary fire of pure love, like the fiery heavenly creatures of Ezekiel. It is accompanied by a communication of humility, as from the source, i.e. that kingdom of heaven which declared in a paradox of divine vitality: "I am meek and lowly of heart." Dante does not suggest that he has already achieved a state of humility and pure love; the whole point is that they are unusually summoned up in him by the girl's greeting. To discover the method by which they become habitual and essential is the aim of the

grand experiment, and was at least one of the
themes of his imagination; to find the point of
change of stress, and therefore of significance, so
that at the end of the *Comedy* Beatrice properly
turns her eyes away from him.

> *Così orai; ed ella sì lontana,*
> *come parea, sorrise e riguardommi;*
> *poi si tornò all'eterna fontana.*

> Thus I prayed; seeming so far,
> she smiled and she gazed back,
> then turned to the eternal spring.

Dante does similarly; he begins to lose consciousness even of her as the full immingled zones
of beatitude open; the early refusal of the salutation which had been "the loss of my beatitude"
and an agony is now the very pulse of the final
exaltation. In what sense, if ever, Beatrice looks
at him again is a thing for consideration only in a
more detailed study of the *Comedy*, from the other
end of the Paradise.

The second incident is more allegorical, but the
allegory is almost a symbolism; that is, it has
almost not a likeness but an identity. Dante one
day sees another young woman coming along.
The whole of the *New Life* is full of other young
women, but, whatever they may have been in his
life, they are in his imagination part of the
inclusiveness of the exclusive thing; they are very

necessary and quite unimportant—what one might call a general sex-awareness without credibility. This one is the lover of one of his friends; her name is Giovanna or Joan; she is so lovely that she has been nicknamed Primavera or Spring. Beatrice was coming at a little distance behind. Love then said to Dante: "If you consider her first name, it is as much as to say *Primavera,* for her name Giovanna is from that Giovanni which preceded the true light, saying: 'I am the voice of one crying in the wilderness. Prepare the way of the Lord' . . . He who is willing to consider with subtlety would call Beatrice Love, for the great similarity she has to me." It would be perhaps unsafe to do so; if by Love is meant the passion of goodwill and humility. But it would be safe to call her the Mother of Love in the soul. The comparison of Giovanna with the Precursor, with that John who preceded *"la verace luce",* makes her the precursor of the divine light which in Beatrice radiates, as was said in the *Banquet,* "with less hindrance". The Divine Thing of goodwill and humility which Dante had experienced springs from his experience of Beatrice; she is the Mother of the grace, and even therefore of the occult God. It is a result of the Incarnation that opened all potentialities of the knowledge of the kingdom of heaven in and through matter. "My covenant shall be in your flesh."

The third point can only be mentioned; it is the death of Beatrice. No doubt, of Beatrice, assuming Beatrice; the fact need not be denied because it means a great deal more than itself. For nothing seems to be more certain than that the original glory, the *Beatricianness* of Beatrice, does either disappear or at least modify itself. In this also we have an exclusive-inclusive event. Beatrice dies; that is the exclusive. The light and beatitude disappear; that is the inclusive. In the imagination the two need not be hostile, nor in fact. "The City is widowed," says Dante, quoting Jeremiah. It is apt to be a blow.

When she returns she comes as a judgement. But also her own nature is more particularly declared. It is declared in a very different kind of poem. But what is declared there is in accord with all that had gone before. The first encounter with Beatrice had awakened physical, mental, and spiritual awareness; later encounters had communicated to Dante moments of humility and pure love, however far he might be from staying in them; she had followed Giovanna as Christ followed John. And she dies, and things happen, and this and the other interferes, and Dante in imagination comes to himself in a savage wood, at the foot of a great hill. The hill is "the cause and occasion of all joy". He tries to climb; he is driven back by the whole of human life understood in its three great images of the gay and beautiful Leopard of youth, the strong and haughty Lion of middle-age, and the terrible insatiable Wolf of old age. These which make up Time, or make up at least all of Time that matters to Dante, drive him back from that mountain which seems to arise beyond Time into a place which seems also to lie beyond Time, the place *"dove il sol tace"*, where the sun is silent, where even Virgil seems but a faint ghost. Virgil is—Virgil, but he is (because of that) poetry, wisdom, institutions, the things that in fact he had been in the world when the great organization of the Empire was formed: all—except the Incarnation. Dante imagines himself here as not able to move on the direct way, as he had in an earlier book imagined Beatrice as dying. He has to go round, through the knowledge of sin and the hellish people "who have lost the good of intellect". He has to find another way to the mountain, but when he comes to the ascent he still approaches it under the light of Venus, the dawn star, "the fair planet which heartens to love". He has to go through the purging of all sins—especially (he says) of pride. He has to listen to the great discourse of Virgil on the nature of love and the terrible malignancy of the sin which is envy and jealousy and pride. He comes, at the top of the mountain, to the Earthly Paradise of Eden; he sees the procession breaking out of the air, the procession which is the "Pageant of the Church". But the final figure of the Pageant of the Church is Beatrice,—it is, in fact, a pageant of Beatrice. He sees her; he feels *"d'antico amor . . . la gran potenza"*; he feels the hot embers *"dell' antica fiamma,"* and he

is answered with what has been called almost the
greatest line in Dante and therefore in all poetry:

Guardaci ben: ben sem, ben sem, Beatrice.
Look well: we are, indeed we are, Beatrice.

It is afterwards that he paradisally recovers the
perfect knowledge of the good, by drinking of
Lethe which removes the knowledge of evil as
evil, by drinking of Eunoe which communicates
the knowledge of good (even evil) as good.
Between the two he sees Beatrice facing the two-
natured Gryphon of Christ, and he sees in her
eyes the reflection of those two natures. Those
eyes are not different; they are the very eyes "from
which Love began to shoot his arrows at you."
Here, surrounded by angels, prophets, evangelists,
virtues, Romantic Love is seen to mirror the
Humanity and Deity of the Redeemer. He sees
it; "my soul tasted the food which makes hungry
where most it satisfies"—so to combine two
poets. It is then that he enters the first heaven
where Piccarda, asked if she does not envy those
in greater heavens their more glorious fate,
answers: "Brother, our will is quiet in the strength
of love . . . here love is fate." All the exchanges
of heaven lie open.

But really, though he now imagined it more
clearly and more strongly, he had not known
anything different, in essence or in principle, when
the face of the Florentine girl flashed her "good

morning" at him along the street of their City.

The chance of a phrase joins the theology of Romantic Love to the theology of the Church. In the *New Life*, at one point, Beatrice snubs Dante; she "denies him her salutation". She had, he says, heard "outrageous rumours" about him. After this Love appeared to him in a vision, and said, *"Ego tamquam centrum circuli cui simili modo se habent circumferentiæ partes; tu autem non sic."* Love refused to explain this, but without presuming to do what Love would not do, one may at least remark that Dante had experienced humility and goodwill through the salutation. When the salutation was refused, he was plunged into anything but humility and goodwill; his beatitude was denied. But Love itself is not so subjected to outward wants. I do not press that Love should here be taken as allegorically equal to Christ; I am inclined to think that this develops in the *New Life* but is certainly not there at the beginning. But Love is certainly sufficiently full of *caritas* to know that he himself is in the centre and unaffected by such things on the circumference of experience as salutations and responses; only with Dante it is not so, or not yet.

About the same time Bonaventura was writing that God was a circle whose centre was everywhere and its circumference nowhere. The diagram of process is clear. Dante is on the circumference, and the things that happen there make a difference to him; he has with them no fixed and always equal relation: only he sees the centre. The Love of the *New Life* is in the centre; to it all parts of the circumference, all times, all experiences, have this equal relation. In humility and good will Dante answered *Love* when things went well, but Love answers *Love* however things go. But beyond that is the state when there is, in effect, no circumference; or rather, every point of the circumference is at the centre, for the circumference itself is *caritas*, and relation is only between the centre and the centre. This is love-in-heaven.

I have said that I have taken these things—so few of so many—from Dante because they are the expressions of the greatest European poet (greatest as poet, not only as metaphysician) and because no one else has given us so complete an exposition of the Way of Romantic Love. It is, of course, in his own terms; the Way can be followed though the terms are rejected. But at least the Way understood in other terms must not be less than his. It is possible to follow this method of love without introducing the name of God. But it is hardly possible to follow it without proposing and involving as an end a state of *caritas* of the utmost possible height and breadth, nor without allowing to matter a significance and power which (of all the religions and philosophies) only Christianity has affirmed.

If, however, we retain the name and idea of

God, and if there is any common agreement about
the state of exalted experience known as the state
of "falling in love", then it is possible to go
further and relate that experience to the Incarnation of the kingdom. When Messias said: "Behold
my mother" he was, in this relation, merely
accurate. The beloved (male or female) is seen
in the light of a Paradisal knowledge and experience of good. Christ exists in the soul, in joy, in
terror, in a miracle of newness. *Ecce, omnia nova
facio.* He who is the mystical child of the lovers
sustains and supports them: they are the children
of their child. "We speak that we do know and
testify that we have seen. . . . No man hath
ascended up into heaven, but he that came down
from heaven, even the Son of Man which is in
heaven."

A theology of this kind will be at the disad-
vantage of all other kinds of theology, and give
rise (within itself) to heresies. Extremists of one
kind will claim for the beloved a purity as non-
existent as the purity of the Church militant upon
earth. Her, or his, humanity is an extremely
maculate humanity, and all the worship under
heaven ought not to prevent her lover from
knowing (with reasonable accuracy and unreason-
able love) when she is lazy, lewd, or malicious.
She has a double nature, and he can have double
sight. On the other hand it will be supposed that
the death of Beatrice implies the non-existence
of Beatrice; that the disappearance of the glory

implies the falsity of the glory. A similar disappearance has not been supposed to invalidate
the fact and authority of Christ, and the quiet
piety—often the extremely quiet piety—of
Christians has (justly) been permitted to relate
itself to the glory of the Transfiguration. The
"quiet affection" of so many prophecies by the
aged might be allowed a similar relation. Quiet
piety and quiet affection have their place in the
kingdom, but we need not force on them an
imperialism they never ought to have at the
expense of other more vivid forms of glory and
of grace. Nor can the denial or disparagement of
those who have forgotten or not experienced it
diminish its authority.

It is perhaps a pity that the clergy as a whole
are so often among the disparagers. A natural
hesitation over the uncovenanted graces leads
them not so much to say wrong things as to say
the right things in the wrong tone. Their proper
concern with one rule of morality leads them to
be careless of another. The Divine Thing that
made itself the foundation of the Church does not
seem, to judge by his comments on the religious
leaders of his day, ever to have hoped much from
officers of a church. The most he would do was
to promise that the gates of hell should not *prevail*
against it. It is about all that, looking back on the
history of the Church, one can feel they have not
done.

Hell has made three principal attacks on the

Way of Romantic Love. The dangerous assumptions produced are: (1) the assumption that it will naturally be everlasting; (2) the assumption that it is personal; (3) the assumption that it is sufficient. Similar dangers have attacked other ways in the kingdom; the instance will be remembered of the London churchwarden who had always supposed himself to be a true Christian until one day he realized, in a flash of clarity, that Christ was dogmatically asserted to have died for all men —especially some few whom he strongly disliked and others whom he extremely despised. He therefore with great good sense, abandoned his profession of Christianity in favour of a free hand with his emotions.

(1). The assumption that the Beatrician state is everlasting is false. "The right faith is that we believe and confess" that it is eternal but is not everlastingly visible, any more than the earthly life of Christ. Its quality may deceive hasty imagination, and it may be expected to return quickly as was Christ by the Church. It may not. Its authority remains unimpaired. The emotional vows, however, springing from its original state, do not at all times appear so possible or desirable. On the other hand, it seems to be true that there is at first a very strong desire in the two lovers to maintain and conduct for ever this experiment towards *caritas* between themselves, and certainly some kind of pledged fidelity would seem to be a condition of the experiment. The Church has

maintained that (under certain conditions) exchanged vows of this kind should be regarded as
final. It has even maintained (justly) that, as in
certain cases, the state of love leads to marriage,
so marriage can lead to a more advanced state of
love, and since, on the whole hypothesis, this is
the only desirable thing, it may be right in its
discipline. (The natural tendency to falsify evidence in favour of a point of view does not perhaps
prevail more strongly here than elsewhere.) But
the matter of marriage is a subject different from
the present and of too lofty a nature to be contented with a paragraph. The appearance of the
glory is temporary; the authority of the glory
towards pure love is everlasting; the quality of the
glory is eternal, such as the heavens have in Christ.

(2). The second assumption is that the state of
love is a personal possession; that is, (i) that it is
the personal adornment of the beloved; (ii) that
it belongs personally to the lover. This mistake
is hardly possible in the first state of humility. But
the fallen state of man produces—again as in
religion—something remarkably like a tendency to
regard the revelation and the glory as one's own
private property. Once the emotions have yielded
to that falsity, the intellect too often is either
thwarted or even betrayed into supporting them.
Until a state of sanctity has been achieved, there
will no doubt always be something proud or
possessive in our attitude towards the thing that
is called love. But, on the whole hypothesis, love

does not belong to lovers, but they to it. It is their
job, as it is their direction, and salvation. It is for
this reason that all such sins as envy and jealousy
are mortal. Jealousy does not mean only sex-
jealousy; it need not even relate to the lovers at all.
Once the authority of the glory has been admitted,
all jealousy and envy are against the idea of and the
way to *caritas*, but the "all" must include the
sexual. One can hardly keep jealousy out of the
office but let it in to the home. It is, always and
everywhere, idolatry; it is a desire to retain the
glory for oneself, which means that one is not
adoring the glory but only one's own relation to
the glory. It ought perhaps, for fear of misunder-
standing, to be added that the strictest mono-
gamist ought to disapprove of jealousy as strongly
as anyone else; the two things are entirely separate.
But it must be admitted that we might be a little
nearer, intellectually, to pure love, if jealousy had
been as passionately denounced as divorce in the
Christian Church. The envious man identifies the
kingdom with himself, and by a frantic effort to
retain the outward manifestation of the kingdom
destroys it in himself, and with it his capacity to
see it outside himself. A sin which is, by its
essence, destructive of goodwill is worse than a sin
which need not be, in its essence, more than dis-
ordered goodwill. Virgil proclaimed the difference; the one kind are bewailed in the place where
they dwell who have lost the good of intellect, the
other in the secular terraces of the Mountain of

Purgatory. There is but one permissible state to any who have seen love: *una fiamma di caritade,* "a flame of love".

(3). The third assumption is even easier than the others: that it is sufficient to have known that state of love. A kind of Calvinism seizes the emotions; the heart has recognized the attributed perfection and stops there. It feels as if of the elect, and it goes on feeling that till it ceases to feel anything. It may recognize a social duty to be useful to others, to feed the poor. "Though I give all my goods . . . and have not charity it profiteth me nothing." To be in love must be followed by the will to *be* love; to be love to the beloved, to be love to all, to be in fact (as the Divine Thing said) perfect.

The alternative is to become the Sir Willoughby Patternes of the spiritual life, and more unbearable even than Meredith's original. Shakespeare gave us the healthy opposite and limit in that as in so much (he, the everlasting corrector of the follies of the disciples of Dante); in our consciousness of such things as regards ourselves we had better not go further than the point at which "with a pure blush we may come off withal".

But, independent of any personal error, the vision has remained. It is not limited to love between the sexes, nor to any love. The use of the word (so spoilt has it become) in some sense colours it with the horrid tint of a false adoration and a pseudo-piety. But grace remains grace whatever fruits are grown from it. The experience of communicated humility and goodwill is the experience of the grace of reality and of the kingdom. The kingdom came down from heaven and was incarnate; since then and perhaps (because of it) before then, it is beheld through and in a carnality of joy. The beloved—person or thing— becomes the Mother of Love; Love is born in the soul; it may have its passion there; it may have its resurrection. It has its own divine nature united with our undivine nature. In such a doctrine the Gospels take on other meanings. The light that lighteth every man is seen without as well as within. But that, by definition, is the nature of the kingdom.

CHAPTER VI

The Practice of Substituted Love

AMONG the epigrams of the kingdom which
St. John arranged in his Gospel immediately
before the triumph of the kingdom, he attributed
to Messias the saying: "Greater love hath no man
than this that a man lay down his life for his
friends." It is, on a second glance, a doubtful
truth. Many men have exhibited their will of love
in such a surrender, but many—perhaps more—
have exercised among all kinds of hardship a
steady tenderness of love besides which the other
seems almost easy. But the phrase has to be
understood in the context of other meanings. The
"greater love" is distinguished by the "laying
down the life": something similar had been
decreed at Sinai: "thou shalt not see my face, for
there shall no man see me and live." The definition does not, in the Gospels, necessarily mean
physical death, even if that is sometimes involved.
When Messias said: "Whosoever will lose his life
for my sake and the Gospel's, the same shall find
it", he did not confine the promise to the martyrs
nor deny to St. John what he allowed to St. James.
Martyrdom might or might not happen. St. Paul,
in the passage already quoted, denied any value

at all to martyrdom unless it were accompanied by *caritas:* "though I give my body to be burned and have not charity, it profiteth me nothing." According to the Apostle, self-sacrifice by itself was as remote from the way of salvation as self-indulgence. As a technique, as a discipline, as a method, it might be useful: no more. But so may —if not self-indulgence at least things gratifying to the self. We are not to deny to others the means of their love because those means may seem to indulge us. "Neither Jew nor Greek, but a new creature." Neither self-sacrifice, as such, nor self-gratification, as such; both may be sacraments of love at any moment, but neither is covenanted. The denial of the self affects both. "It is no more I that live, but Christ that liveth in me" is the definition of the pure life which is substituted for both.

The taunt flung at that Christ, at the moment of his most spectacular impotency, was: "He saved others; himself he cannot save." It was a definition as precise as any in the works of the medieval schoolmen. It had been already accepted by the action—the action which restrained action—of Messias, as it had been accepted still earlier by his words when he chose necessity. It was an exact definition of the kingdom of heaven in operation, and of the great discovery of substitution which was then made by earth. Earth, at best till then under the control of law, had to find that no law was enough unless the burden of the law, of the

law kept or the law unkept, could be known to be
borne by heaven in the form of the Holy Thing
that came down from heaven. Earth had to find
also that the new law of the kingdom made that
substitution a principle of universal exchange.
The first canon of substitution had been declared
in the myth of origin ages before, when the law
of man's responsibility for man had been shaped.
It had denounced there the first-born child of the
Adam, though of the Adam no longer in the union
of the knowledge of the good, but in the divided
sorrow of conception and of work. The child was
Cain, the incarnation of their union outside
Paradise, and in some sense of the self-desirous
spirit which troubles the divine glory in all lovers.
An opposition to goodness was in his nature and
is in theirs, a desire to trouble goodness with some
knowledge of some kind of evil. He not only
killed his brother; he also made an effort to carry
on the intellectual falsity which his parents had
experienced when they fled from facts in their
new shame. He became rhetorical—it is, so early,
the first appearance of a false style of words: "Am
I my brother's keeper?" It is a question asked by
most people at some moment. "The voice of thy
brother's blood crieth unto me from the ground."
That answer became a law in the covenants: "At
the hand of every man's brother will I require the
life of man." As the single tyranny of Cain
developed into the social tyranny in Egypt and in
Israel itself, so the law gathered round itself the

clamour of the prophets for social justice: "seek judgement, relieve the oppressed, judge the fatherless, plead for the widow . . . what mean ye that ye beat my people to pieces, and grind the faces of the poor? saith the Lord God of hosts." Under the organized effort of Rome towards at least something of the Virgilian equity, this had been defined in the moral duty of all classes and individuals declared by the Precursor; it had become the gospel of the Precursor as of Virgil, except that the one gospel expected beyond itself what the other hardly could. Messias had shown that he would demand and assume its fulfilment by all who wished to follow his own gospel. It had to be left, then, to men to choose or not to choose. The direct concern of the new kingdom was with other things, with the love that had substituted itself for men, and with the love between men that was to form itself after the manner of that original love.

When Messias removed his visibility, he left behind him a group of united followers; he had created the Church. The Church, as such, will be the subject of other volumes of the series, and is not to be discussed at length here. If the Acts of the Apostles are any guide—say in chapters ii, iii, iv—the Church began with direct statements of dogma and direct communication of rites. Necessarily, as it spread, it had to organize itself; it had to make decisions on fundamental questions. There was the question, as it grew, of what on certain points it did actually believe; it answered this by finding out in its Councils what in fact it did—in its various localities—actually believe. The message of the Councils to the localities after an inquiry tended to be not so much "we are telling you what is true" as "it has been decided that *this* is what the Church actually believes." Certainly, by rapid development of a hypothesis of its nature, the two things became identical, but there was a difference in method and indeed in idea. Occasionally a Council came to a decision which was not accepted, in which case the hypothesis sooner or later involved the view that it was not a proper Council. For the hypothesis was that there was operative within the Church the sacred and eternal reconciliation of all things, which the Church did not and could not deserve. The Church (it was early decided) was not an organization of sinless men but of sinful, not a union of adepts but of less than neophytes, not of *illuminati* but of those that sat in darkness. Nevertheless, it carried within it an energy not its own, and it knew what it believed about that energy. It was the power of the Reconciler, and the nature of the Reconciler was of eternity as of time, of heaven as of earth, of absolute God as of essential Man. "Let those who say *There was when he was not* be anathema."

There was then, so to put it, a new way, the way of return to blissful knowledge of all things. But this was not sufficient; there had to be a new self to go on the new way. This was the difficulty of the Church then as it is now, as it always is after any kind of conversion. There are always three degrees of consciousness, all infinitely divisible: (i) the old self on the old way; (ii) the old self on the new way; (iii) the new self on the new way. The second group is the largest, at all times and in all places. It is the frequent result of romantic love. It forms, at any one moment, the greatest part of the visibility of the Church, and, at most moments, practically all of oneself that one can know, for the new self does not know itself. It consists of the existence of the self, unselfish perhaps, but not yet denied. This self often applies itself unselfishly. It transfers its actitivies from itself as a centre to its belief as a centre. It uses its angers on behalf of its religion or its morals, and its greed, and its fear, and its pride. It operates on behalf of its notion of God as it originally operated on behalf of itself. It aims honestly at better behaviour, but it does not usually aim at change; and perhaps it was in relation to that passionate and false devotion that Messias asked: "Think ye when the Son of Man cometh he shall find faith upon the earth?"

Those who accuse the Church accuse it—justly —of not being totally composed of new selves; those who defend it defend it—justly—as being a new way. No doubt, the old self on the new way is a necessary period, in most cases, of change. But the Apostles, to judge by the epistles, were not willing that the faithful should remain consistently faithful to themselves. They demanded, as Messias had demanded, that the old self should deny itself. It was to be removed and renovated, to be a branch of the vine, a point of the pattern. It was to become an article of love. And what then is love?

It is possible here to follow only one of the many definitions the New Testament holds; the definition of death. To love is to die and live again; to live from a new root. Part of the experience of romantic love has been precisely that; the experience of being made new, the "renovation" of nature, as Dante defined it in a particular experience of love. That experience is not sufficient to maintain itself, or at least does not choose to do so. But what is there experienced, and what has been otherwise experienced by many in religion, or outside religion, has to be followed by choice. "Many are called but few are chosen": we are called from the kingdom but we choose from ourselves. The choice is to affect not only our relation with God but our relation with men. There is to be something of the same kind of relation in it. "These things have I spoken unto you, that my joy might remain in you, and that your joy might be full." It is odd how rarely Messias is seen as full of joy—but there it is. He said so; no one else. He proceeded towards our joy: "This is my commandment, that ye love one another, as I have loved you." The First Epistle

of St. John carried the same idea, and the Revised
Version has it more sharply than the Authorized.
"Hereby know we love, because he laid down his
life for us, and we ought also to lay down our lives
for the brethren . . . if we love one another, God
abideth in us, and his love is perfected in us." We
are to love each other *as* he loved us, laying down
our lives *as* he did, that this love may be perfected.
We are to love each other, that is, by acts of
substitution. We are to be substituted and to bear
substitution. All life is to be vicarious—at least,
all life in the kingdom of heaven is to be vicarious.
The difference between life in the kingdom and
life outside the kingdom is to be this. "Except
your righteousness exceed the righteousness of the
Scribes and Pharisees, ye shall in no wise enter
into the kingdom of Heaven." But many of the
Scribes and Pharisees were good and holy men?
yes; what then? it is this love-in-substitution, this
vicarious life, which is no more in their law than
in the gospel of the Precursor. "Go, tell John,
the blind receive their sight . . . the least in the
kingdom of heaven is greater than he."

It has been the habit of the Church, since the
earliest times, ostentatiously to use some such
substitution, in one rite at least: in the baptism
of infants. It is understood that this is largely due
to the persecutions, but also to the nature of the
sacrament itself; which was purposed for infants
as well as adults, and yet demanded penitence and
faith before its operation could be insured. This

responsibility was laid on the godparents: "at the hand of every man's brother will I require the life of man". But it is others than infants who can swear more sincerely and more humbly by others' mouths than ever by their own, though it must be with the agreement and desire of their own. It is one of the difficulties of the Church that her presentation of experience does not always coincide with realized experience. The conversion she demands and the sustenance she communicates come sometimes from alien and even from hostile sources; it is one conversion and one sustenance with hers. The invisible Church moves in another manner than the visible; indeed the invisible must include that earthly scepticism opposition which the visible Church so greatly needs and yet cannot formally include. The sponsors in baptism exhibit the idea of substitution, as that habit which existed in the early Church of being baptized "for the dead" exhibited it. Part of the fact which such an exhibition ritually and sacramentally presents is the making a committal of oneself from another's heart and by another's intention. It is simpler sometimes and easier, and no less fatal and blessed, to do it so; to surrender and be offered to destiny by another rather than by oneself; it is already a little denial of the self.

But that is as holy Luck may decide. Whatever the means of beginning, the life itself is vicarious. The courtesies of that life are common enough—to lend a book, for example, is a small motion in it, an article of the web of glory. It is the full principle which is defined by the New Testament, and the making of contracts on that principle which exhibit, in the denial of self, the pattern of the web.

St. Paul, in one of those letters which are at once mystical diaries, archiepiscopal charges, and friendly messages, threw out an instruction to the Church at Galatia (Gal. vi. 2). "Bear ye one another's burdens, and so fulfil the law of Christ." It is, like the patience of Job, one of our most popular texts. In exterior things it is recognized as valid—at least until we become bored; the fiftieth rather than the first visit to the sick is distasteful. Interiorly, it is less frequently supposed to be possible, and even exteriorly it has a wider range than is, perhaps, allowed. St. Paul's injunction is to such acts as "fulfil the law of Christ", that is, to acts of substitution. To take over the grief or the fear or the anxiety of another is precisely that; and precisely that is less practised than praised. "Mystical substitution" we have heard from the text-books, or from other books that are less than the text-books. It is supposed to be for "nuns, confessors, saints, not us": so much the worse for us. We are supposed to be content to "cast our burdens on the Lord". The Lord indicated that the best way to do so was to hand these over to someone else to cast, or even to cast them on him in someone else. There will still be work enough for the self, carrying the burdens of others, and becoming the point at which those burdens are taken over by the Divine Thing which is the kingdom: "as he is, even so are we in this world".

The technique needs practice and intelligence, as much intelligence as is needed for any other business contract. The commerce of love is best established by commercial contracts with man. If we are to make agreements with our adversaries quickly, we ought to be even quicker to make them with our friends. Any such agreement has three points: (i) to know the burden; (ii) to give up the burden; (iii) to take up the burden. It is perhaps in this sense also that Messias said: "Deny the self, take up the cross, follow me"; it being admitted and asserted that the crucifixion itself is his. He flung out those two seemingly contradictory assertions, he who was rich in contradictions: "take up the cross", "my yoke is easy, and my burden is light." It is not till the cross has been lifted that it can be a burden. It is in the exchange of burdens that they become light. But the carrying of a cross may be light because it is not to the crucifixion. It is "of faith" that that is done; that is, it is the only part of the work still to be done that we should be fitted into the state where all is done, into the kingdom and the knowledge of everything as good. But a pride and self-respect which will be content to repose upon Messias is often unapt to repose on "the brethren."

Yet that too is part of the nature of all and of the action of the contract. The one who gives has to remember that he has parted with his burden, that it is being carried by another, that his part is to believe that and be at peace; "brother, our will is quiet in the strength of love . . . herein love is fate." The one who takes has to set himself—mind and emotion and sensation—to the burden, to know it, imagine it, receive it—and sometimes not to be taken aback by the swiftness of the divine grace and the lightness of the burden. It is almost easier to believe that Messias was probably right about the mysteries of the Godhead than that he was merely accurate about the facts of everyday life. One expects the burden always to be heavy, and it is sometimes negligible; which is precisely what he said. Discovering that, one can understand more easily the happy abuse he flung at the disciples, say, at the two who went to Emmaus. "Then he said unto them, O fools and slow of heart to believe all that the prophets have spoken: ought not Christ to have suffered these things and have entered into his glory? And beginning at Moses and all the prophets he expounded unto them in all the scriptures the things concerning himself."

The giver's part may be harder than the taker's; that is why, here, it may be more blessed to give than to receive, though in the equity of the kingdom there is little difference. It has a greater tendency towards humility and the intellectual

denial of the self. In all the high pagan
philosophies, now as then, there are many great
virtues, and their leaders and teachers often were
and are holy and humble men of heart. I do not
remember that any of them cried out: "See how
meek and lowly I am!" No Christian has been
encouraged to murmur of himself in that state
which is called "the inner chamber" what Christ
proclaimed of himself to the world. It is the
everlasting difference between the gospel of
Christ as one who is to be imitated and one who
is to be believed, between one who is an example
of living and one who is the life itself; between
the philosophies that advise unselfishness as the
best satisfaction in life and the religion that
asserts exchange to be the only possible means of
tolerable life at all. The denial of the self has
become metaphysical. He came to turn the world
upside-down, and no one's self-respect will stand
for that. It is habitual to us therefore to prefer
to be miserable rather than to give, and to believe
that we can give, our miseries up.

There is, of course, a technique. If A is to
carry B's burden he must be willing to do it to
the full, even though he may not be asked to do
it to the full. It is easy to sentimentalize, but the
Day of Judgement exhibits our responsibilities
in each case: "at the hand of every man's brother
will I require . . ." Messias may, now, carry
the burden if we ourselves deliberately neglect or
forget the agreement, but the lucidity of the good

knowing the evil as good is likely to exhibit the negligence or forgetfulness as much as the substitution of himself. It is therefore necessary (a) not to take burdens too recklessly; (b) to consider exactly how far any burden, accepted to the full, is likely to conflict with other duties. There is always a necessity for intelligence.

Our reluctance is inevitably encouraged by the difficulty of carrying out this substitution in the physical world; of developing between men the charismatic ministry. The body is probably the last place where such interchange is possible; it is why Messias deigned to heal the body "that ye may know that the Son of Man hath power *on earth* to forgive sins." No such exchange is possible where any grudge—of pride, greed or jealousy—exists, nor any hate; so far all sins must have been "forgiven" between men. In some states of romantic love it is felt that the power of healing exists, if only it could be brought into action, and on the basis of Romantic Theology it could so be brought into action. We habitually expect too little of ourselves. But it is not only in states of realization that the power exists. It is limited, peculiarly, by other duties. Most men are already so committed that they ought not, whatever their goodwill, to contemplate the carrying of the burden of paralysis or consumption or even lesser things. They are still bound to prefer one good to another. Certainly it is reasonable to believe that the kind of burden might be transmuted into another equivalent kind, and in a full state of the kingdom upon earth such a transmutation would be agreeable and natural. It remains at present an achievement of which our "faith" is not yet capable. That is no reason why we should not practise faith, a faith in the interchange of the kingdom operating in matter as out of matter, because whatever distinction there may be between the two is only a distinction between modes of love.

It is natural that, in certain happy states (e.g., the Beatrician love), there should be a desire to make any contract of the kind mutual, and so it often may be. At the same time the tendency is sometimes for the pattern not to return but to proceed. The old proverb said that there was always one who kissed and one who took kisses; that too, accepted, is in this sense a part of the pattern. The discovery that one cannot well give back or be given back what one has given or been given in the same place is sometimes as painful as the discovery that one is being loved on principle and not from preference: a good deal of conviction of the equality of all points in the web of the kingdom and of the denial of the self is necessary to make it bearable. Man—fallen man —has, oddly, the strongest objection to being the cause of the practice of *caritas* by someone else. Yet the Apostles in their epistles continually, and necessarily, exhort the faithful to the practice of such a submission: "let us not love in word,

neither in tongue, but in deed and in truth." To
be grateful for what one does not want is a step
towards love, even if it is the rather difficult
gratitude for the smirk of a well-meaning intercession by the official twice-born in the visible
Church. Gratitude is a necessity of all life; it is
love looking at the past as faith is love intending
the future, and hope is the motion of the shy
consciousness of love in the present self; and
gratitude, like love, is its own sufficiency:

>   the grateful mind
> By owing owes not but still pays, at once
> Indebted and discharged.

It is with the intention of substituted love that
all "intercessory" prayer must be charged, and
with care that there is no intention of emotional
bullying. Even prayer for the conversion of others
is apt to be more like prayer for their conversion
to the interceder's own point of view than to the
kingdom. The old self on the new way has always
enjoyed himself most at prayer. He can pray
fervently for other people's delivery from other
people's sins; he can indicate to Messias where X
is wrong; he can try and bring supernatural power
to bear on X to stop him or divert him or
encourage. It is precisely because he is playing
with a real power that this is so dangerous. It is
dangerous, for example, to pray that Nero may
be delivered from killing Agrippina; it looks a
fairly safe petition but . . . What do we know of

Nero, of Agrippina, of Messias? But it can never be dangerous, without particularizing, without fluency, intensely to recollect Nero and Agrippina "in the Lord", nor can it be dangerous to present all pains and distresses to the kingdom with the utmost desire that Messias may be, and the recollection that at that moment he is, the complete reconciliation—through the point that prays, if conditions are so, but if not then through all and any of the points of the kingdom.

"All and any." We operate, mostly, in sequence, but sequence is not all. "I am Alpha and Omega, the first and the last, the beginning and the end." There is no space here to discuss theories of time or the nature of the intercession of the saints. The vicarious life of the kingdom is not necessarily confined to sequence even among the human members of the kingdom. The past and the future are subject to interchange, as the present with both, the dead with the living, the living with the dead. "The living creatures ran and returned, as the appearance of a flash of lightning." The laying down of the life is not confined, in the universal nature of the Sole-Begotten, to any points of space or time. It flashes and returns, in a joy, in a distress, and often without joy or distress. Along such threads the glory runs, and along what are, at present, even fainter threads than those. The method of the new life which Messias (he said) came to give so abundantly begins with substitution and proceeds by substi-

tution. No such substitution accents the individual
less; on the contrary, it is, for most, the strongest
life of the individual. Even in the kingdom of this
world those are greatest who (rightly or wrongly)
have had assessed to them the desires, wills, lives
of others, when Cæsar was Rome and Napoleon
was France. It is the touch of impersonality in
Cæsar, the hint that he had in his own strange
way denied the self and become only Cæsar even
to himself that makes him so fascinating. His
star burns on the ancient world, as Virgil saw it
at Actium, over the homes, the families, the
pietas of man, before it is answered by the other
star that proclaimed the kingdom of a greater
substitution.

In the old days David, or whoever wrote the
Psalm, exclaimed that no man could redeem
or give a ransom for his brother, and in the
ultimate sense that is so still, but it was said
before the revelation of the secret of evil known
as good, and before the mystery of the Atonement of Messias had brought all things into the
pattern of the Atonement. All goodness is from
that source, changed and exchanged in its process.
It was said of the Friars that one went patched
for another's rending, and in the kingdom men
go glorious for others' labours, and all grown
glorious from the labour of all. Messias, after
he had spoken to the astonished soul of the five
husbands that she had had, and none of them all
he—no, not the present lover, however righteous,

however holy, he—spoke yet more riddles to the
returning Apostles. He looked on the fields, he
saw them white to harvest, he cried out of wages
and fruit and eternal life, and at once of him
that sowed and him that reaped and their
common joy. And even as he said it, he flung
his words into a wider circuit: "herein is that
saying true, one soweth and another reapeth.
I sent you to reap that whereon ye bestowed no
labour: other men laboured and ye are entered
into their labours." What! after self-sacrifice
and crosses and giving up goods and life, the
mind perplexed, the heart broken, the body
wrecked—is there not a little success of our own,
our own in him, of course, but at least his in us?
None; "I sent you to reap that whereon ye
bestowed no labour." The harvest is of others,
as the beginning was in others, and the process
was by others. This man's patience shall adorn
that man, and that man's celerity this; and
magnificence and thrift exchanged; and chastity
and generosity; and tenderness and truth, and so
on through the kingdom. We shall be graced by
one and by all, only never by ourselves; the only
thing that can be ours is the fiery blush of the
laughter of humility when the shame of the
Adam has become the shyness of the saints. The
first and final maxim in the present earth is *deny
the self*, but—there or here—when the need for
denial has passed, it may be possible to be
astonished at the self as at everything else, when

that which is God is known as the circle whose
centre is everywhere and the circumference
nowhere. "He saved others; himself he cannot
save." "The glory which thou gavest me I have
given them; that they may be one, even as we
are one: I in them, and thou in me, that they may
be made perfect in one."

CHAPTER VII

The City

THE coming of the kingdom, in myth, in legend, in law, in history, in morals and metaphysics, has been the coming of a thing at once exclusive of all things and inclusive of everything. All the threads of the pattern have that nature, and the whole pattern is of the same nature.

All the gospels are full of that inclusive-exclusive command to do things "for my sake". It is the definition of *caritas*, and *caritas* is the nature of the kingdom. It is habitually set against *eros*, the personal love, and distinguished as being a kind of impersonal goodwill. If goodwill is taken to mean the *voluntas inflammata*, the fiery wheel of the prophets, it will serve; unfortunately, nothing is less like a fiery wheel than the hob-nailed boots of ordinary moral effort. They are hardly nailed with joy. The Passion of Messias, for all its grief, was accompanied by discourses of delight and joy—at least in the arrangement of the Gospels.

"It is man's duty," said Johnson, "to be happy." It is not enough to be full of an effort towards goodwill unless it is a joyous goodwill. "The Spirit of glory is upon you," said St. Peter, contemplating persecutions and martyrdoms. The very idea—the very distant idea—of more pain and distress than ordinary life supplies is enough to chill the blood in our already pallid happiness. It was the consciousness of the extreme surrender and the sadness which must accompany it that caused one Christian poet to compose a hymn with the refrain:

> Jesus Christ is our Redeemer
> And we wish to God he weren't.

His intelligence was lamentable but his emotion was comprehensible. We are unhappy enough anyhow, and if Christianity is to mean a little more unhappiness, more discipline, more trials—the prospect not unnaturally drives men to that plea for annihilation which (the Church declares) is the only thing the Omnipotence will never grant, except indeed by the annihilation which is he. On the other hand, there is an offensive cheerfulness encouraged by some Christians which is very trying to any person of moderate sensibility. We are to be bright; we are to smile at strangers; we are (last horror of daily life!) to get into conversation with strangers. It is some comfort to reflect that Messias was against our being bright as he was against our being gloomy. He was against our being anything at all. He indicated continually that it was our wish to do or be something by ourselves, even to be saved by ourselves, that was the root of the trouble. It is at least possible for some of us easily to deny ourselves any tendency towards a communal cheerfulness.

The word that runs through the Bible, the word that defines the yonder side of the demanded *caritas*, is glory. It is glory which in the Old Testament from a general brightness becomes a mathematical splendour; it is glory which accompanies, in the New, the first beginning of signs when water is suddenly poured out as wine; it is communicated to the disciples—"the glory which thou gavest me I have given them"; it accompanies the City that slides from the utmost heavens into the sight of Patmos. In the Gospel of St. John the word is particularly associated with action; it is the acts of Messias which form the glory. The first miracle is his glory. He says to Martha just before the raising of Lazarus (in answer to her: "Lord, by this time he stinketh"): "Said I not unto thee, that, if thou wouldest believe, thou shouldst see the glory of God?" He promises the Apostles: "whatsoever ye shall ask in my name, that will I do, that the Father may be glorified in the Son." He looks forward to the Passion: "The hour is come that the Son of Man should be glorified . . . Father, save me from this hour: but for this cause came I unto this hour. Father, glorify thy name." The last discourse is a torrent of glory; the last prayer a declaration of communicated glory, that is, of communicated acts. The pattern of the glory is a pattern of acts.

The fulfilment of all things has been, traditionally, described twice in the Bible: once in the *Song of Solomon*, once in the *Apocalypse*. The first, as has been often pointed out (significantly by Sue in *Jude the Obscure*), is a love-poem or a set of love-poems, or a drama of love (critical opinion is variable); the second is a revolutionary pamphlet. The *Encyclopædia Britannica* says of the first, and might have said of the second, that "its oriental standard of taste differs from that of the modern West." In spite of that, neither book has been without its effect on the modern West, and even on the taste of the modern West. The doves and harts of the one and the sea monster of the other have lingered in our literature and in our thought. More particularly, the "community" has lingered, for in both the mystical tradition has thought of the universal and not of the individual. The chapter-headings of the first refer the passion and the joy not to Christ and the soul but to Christ and the Church; and the very text of the other contains the vision not of the soul apostate or redeemed but of the City. The idea of the kingdom has always had some content of revolution and of love, however conventional and prosaic the visible Church has made them; for the maxim of the kingdom is that of all love and all revolution: *ecce, omnia nova facio*—behold, I make all things new.

"And I saw a new heaven and a new earth . . . and I John saw the holy city . . . descending out of heaven from God, having the glory of God: and her light was like unto a stone most precious, even like a jasper stone, clear as crystal." It is like the "terrible crystal" which was over the heads of the living creatures in Ezekiel; and perhaps it is not entirely irrelevant to think of that crystal as being over the heads of all those great other monsters which loom in vast significances through all such art—the horse of Job among the trumpets, and the Leviathan that is no play-mate for girls, and the camel that is too huge for a needle's eye however enlarged, and the eagles on which in the time of Exodus Israel was to be brought to the Lord. The new earth and the new heaven come like the two modes of knowledge, knowledge being the chief art of love, as love is the chief art of knowledge: earth a directness, heaven a substitution. The City—holding both—is the formulation of that old prophecy—"a kingdom of priests . . . they shall teach no more every man his neighbour, and every man his brother, saying: Know the Lord; for they shall all know me, from the least of them unto the greatest of them, saith the Lord." The same thing is said of the City: "I saw no temple therein . . . the Lord God Almighty and the Lamb are the temple of it . . . the Lord God giveth them light." The centre is everywhere and the circumference nowhere; that is, it is hierarchic and republican at once, as

all good states, even on this present earth, are
known to be, where everything and everyone is
unique and is the subject of due adoration so, and
yet, all being unique, "none is afore or after other,
none is greater or less than another."

Those who are excluded from the City ate
"whoever loveth and maketh a lie." This too is
the intellectual falsity of the beginning, the
"making of aprons" of the myth and the prophets
prophesying falsely of Jeremiah; it is, obviously,
excluded from the City because, anyhow, it cannot
see the City, or if, not as a place to be entered.
"The people who have lost the good of intellect"
cannot exist at the highest point of intellect, the
point where all is brought out into clarity, "with
every secret thing". It is this which has distinguished the doctrines of Christendom; nothing
is to be lost or forgotten; all things are to be
known. They can be known as good, however
evil, for they can be known as occasions of love.
But known they must and shall be: "the Lord
God giveth them light". Messias and the New
Testament know nothing about blotting out the
past. Messias insists on making it prominent. It
is natural to a doctrine which has not hesitated to
make its God responsible for all; responsible in
this sense—that knowing with a clarity inconceivable to man everything that would happen in
his creation he yet ordained the creation. No
amount of pious exposition of the freewill of man
can avoid that fact. There is no split second of

the unutterable horror and misery of the world
that he did not foresee (to use the uselessness of
that language) when he created; no torment of
children, no obstinacy of social wickedness, no
starvation of the innocent, no prolonged and
deliberate cruelty, which he did not know. It is
impossible for the mind of man to contemplate
an infinitesimal fraction of the persistent cruelty
of mankind, and beyond mankind of the animals,
through innumerable years, and yet remain sane.
"The whole creation groaneth and travaileth together in pain." The Omnipotence contemplated
that pain and created; that is, he brought its possibility—and its actuality—into existence. Without him it could not have been; and calling it his
permission instead of his will may be intellectually
accurate, but does not seem to get over the fact
that if the First Cause has power, intelligence,
and will to cause a universe to exist, then he is the
First Cause of it. The First Cause cannot escape
being the First Cause. All the metaphors about
fathers giving their children opportunities to be
themselves fail, as all metaphors fail. Fathers are
not the First Cause. God only is God. The pious
have been—as they always are—too anxious to
excuse him; the prophet was wiser: "I form the
light and create darkness: I make peace and create
evil: I the Lord do all these things."

But other religions have gone so far; Christianity
has gone further. It has proclaimed that the
Omnipotence recognized that responsibility in

the beginning and from the beginning, and acted
on it—not by infusing grace only but by himself
becoming what himself had made, in the condition
to which it had, by his consent, brought itself. It
is this particular act, done of free choice and from
love, which makes the Faith unique. All the
deities, and all the sacrificed deities, the sun-myths
and the vegetable simulacra, all that look much
like the God of Christianity, look in the last
analysis much unlike the God of Christianity.
There is over all of them a Fate, or else there is
no union with man. But Christian dogma has
denied all Fate behind the Omnipotence as Alfred
denied it in his translation of Boethius a thousand
years ago. "But I say, as do all Christian men,
that it is the divine purpose that rules them, not
Fate." It has asserted the indivisible union of the
two natures in the single Person. It has asserted
that this union accepted responsibility; at the hand
of God himself God has required the life of man.

It is from this fact that the City descends to
Patmos and the world. The descent of the City,
in its web of exchanged glory, is the definition of
the necessary *caritas*, the "for my sake" of the
gospels. The stress of love in man has altered.
There is only one reason why anything should
be loved on this earth—because God loves
it. Beatrice (whoever and whatever Beatrice may
be) is no longer to be loved for the gratification of
the lover, in however pure or passionate a sense.
She is no longer to be loved for herself alone;

that is perhaps the height of ordinary inventions of literature, and it was much as is generally suggested. Beatrice anyhow is generally, and naturally, satisfied with that. But the kingdom of heaven is not satisfied. Beatrice is to be loved "for my sake". It sounds simple, and is difficult. It is the change in the laying down of the love and the life, hinted at by those masters of the spiritual way who speak of the soul abandoning the love of created things before she can find God. It is precisely *her* love—her own love of created things—that she abandons, and her own consciousness of love; and she may then, not improperly, when they say to her, "thy mother and thy brethren," look at all things round her and answer, "Behold my mother and my brethren." The law of exchange is the mother of the soul; and this too is that other curious promise of Messias, when he committed himself to the statement that those who had given up anything for his sake should have its equivalent multitudinously restored—as in the book of Job. "Verily I say unto you, There is no man that hath left house, or parents, or brethren, or wife, or children, for the kingdom of God's sake, who shall not receive manifold more in this present time, and in the world to come life everlasting." It has not been generally observed that things seem to happen so, perhaps because there is a heavenly catch in the promise, after all. Messias is certainly to be trusted, but only after his own manner.

"He is his own interpreter," as a once popular hymn justly remarks. He is; no one else could begin to think of his interpretations. "My thoughts are not your thoughts." One cannot object; that is the nature of God, but it makes things more difficult. St. Paul defined the restoration in another epigram: "having nothing, yet possessing all things." It is the custom of the City.

As the acts of Messias are historic and contemporary at once, so the coming of the City is contemporary and future at once. It is to be (the Church has affirmed), but also it is now. There are, now, flashes and hints of a state in which preference has disappeared. Things are merely good, and their only elements are peace and joy. There is no law to control these moments and no guide to direct us to them. They only exist. They have that additional grace that they redeem us from a too specialized imprisonment in a terminology. It is necessary to have words for things, and it is helpful to recognize things by words. It is also possible to come under the tyranny of special forms of words. The thing we call "grace" is here and there and gone and back, like the lightning of the living creatures, and a greater: "so shall also the coming of the Son of Man be." It is a kind of life, and in that life we are for a moment no more ourselves. It is a life admirably described in the Apocalypse as drinking freely of the waters of life in the City, so simple,

so natural, so one with all. It is to that life that
the two images in the Bible of the Consummation
addressed themselves, each at the end of its
utterance. The Shulamite ends: "make haste,
my beloved, and be thou like to a roe or to a young
hart upon the mountains of spices." The witness
in the Apocalypse ends: "He which testifieth these
things saith: Surely I come quickly. Amen. Even
so, come, Lord Jesus."

The organic word of prayer which Messias
conveyed to his disciples unites the City with its
reflections upon earth. The descent from heaven
reaches that prayer, utters it, stays in it, and turns
again in it towards the re-ascent. The living
creatures of heaven run up and down on it,
desiring, with that blaze of intellectual curiosity
characteristic of heaven, to understand the
relations in which they share; and on it also all
sharers of exchange on earth. The prayer opens
with an invocation of beatitude in its provident
relation towards us. It proclaims and invokes the
sanctity of that heaven in all its types upon earth.
The name of God is that which all creation, in
its different kinds and degrees, aspires to know,
to utter, and to become. Its life is in that; all
difference is in the mode of knowledge. It
invokes the kingdom, following on the prophecy
of the Precursor and the royal incantation of
Messias—let it emerge; let the name become the
kingdom and the flashing and glorious moments
of love be a pattern and an order and an instinct

and no less themselves. It entreats for earth the pure and absolute knowledge of earth in the same manner in which that knowledge already exists in the heaven of the eternal beatitude; let us understand the completion even here, the completion of all and of this very event in which we are now engaged, the peace of the determination of the Will as it is already fulfilled. It desires, for that end, the nourishment of all beings, but especially of men, in all states—the bread which is the joy. It touches, then, on a thing which, known to us too bitterly here, is (one way or another) still known in heaven—the ardent interchange of pardon; but now is its grand terror, in a word as short as any in the prayer, in the little monosyllable "as". "Forgive us . . . *as* we forgive . . ." in the manner that . . . to the extent that . . . This is the acceptance of the government of Messias, the assent to the law of interchange, the accommodation of heaven to our intention upon earth. It is at once our humility towards and our control upon heaven; the casting off or the drawing-down of rule and measurement by ourselves and for ourselves. Forgive us *as*— and then the thing, as if startled at its own daring and shocked at its own danger, rushes up into a heavenly fear: "lead us not into temptation." do not abandon us to such a trial: what is the nothingness that is we to do there? deliver us, deliver us from evil, from the evil that man chose once to know, the evil of split knowledge and the agony of the good turned against itself, the evil therefore of the deprivation of good, of the loss of joy, the illusion of love in the self and the monstrous duplicities that follow the self: deliver us, deliver us. "Thou only art holy, thou only art the Lord"; "without thee Nothing is strong——" out of that Nothing deliver us, by ourselves becoming nothing to ourselves, having no power to be except in the kingdom. "For thine is the kingdom"— the three changes of the great transmutation follow; "thine is the kingdom, and the power, and the glory," the web, and the operation down all the threads of the web, and the eternal splendour of threads and web at once. "This also is Thou" —not that we can ever know the glory in itself; at the height of all knowledge, all knowledge drops— "neither is this Thou."

To think of the pattern is not to be part of the pattern; to talk of exchange is not to exchange. The division between the old self and the new is greater than any distinction between the ways, though the ways are important. St. Paul feared the danger that Messias implied: "they who say Lord, Lord, and do not the things that I say"; "lest when I have preached to others, I myself should be a castaway." Christendom has demanded the closest examination of conscience to avoid that retrogression, but our motions slide down, one below the other, and the schism of intention is deeper than any other; where is certainty? who can be sure of any motive in any act? Yet the choice, the wish that may become the will, may be there, whatever our ignorance; to desire to follow the good is important, to desire to follow the good from the good is more important. St. John eased the young Church: "if our hearts condemn us, God is greater than our hearts, and knoweth all things." Messias himself condescended to encouragement in the parable of the tares. "Sow good seed; but when good and evil spring up together, and all a mixed growth in the heart, do not fret, do not go hunting among motives for blades of wheat here and blades of tares there. I will separate all, I will save these and annihilate those; be at peace, be glad, leave decision to me. Only sow; work while it is yet day." In all communicated joy there is the sense of three great sayings. The first is the joyous mockery of Messias: "O fools and slow of heart to believe . . ." The second is his definition: "I am Alpha and Omega, the beginning and the end, the first and the last." The third is the threat which must inevitably accompany the coming of the heavenly thing onto earth: "Blessed is he whosoever shall not be offended at me."